Improving Children's Critical and Creative Thinking Using Media

This book addresses the most common questions raised by parents regarding the impact of media on children. It offers insights on suitable media choices for children, fostering healthy media usage, determining appropriate age for media consumption, and navigating related technologies. Additionally, practical suggestions are provided on integrating media literacy into everyday situations with children.

This book explores theories surrounding the effects of media violence, the importance of teaching online ethics, children's fear toward film characters, shielding children from distressing news, promoting advertisement literacy, exploring media's role in sexual education, and cultivating critical thinking skills to discern media clichés. These topics are thoroughly explored and discussed within the book. By engaging with this book, parents will acquire a practical level of media literacy that empowers them to support their children's growth in critical and creative thinking. It equips parents to navigate the challenges that arise when using both traditional and digital media effectively.

Audiences of this book include parents, caregivers of children, educators, and anyone involved in working with children.

Mania Alehpour is pursuing her second PhD at UNSW. In her current PhD thesis, she is investigating how adolescents use social media to improve their mental health. For her first PhD, she studied children's interpretation of critical concepts in animated movies. Throughout her career, she has focused on various aspects of media and children.

Improving Children's Critical and Creative Thinking Using Media

Through Traditional and Digital Media

Mania Alehpour

LONDON AND NEW YORK

First published 2025
by Routledge
4 Park Square, Milton Park, Abingdon, Oxon OX14 4RN

and by Routledge
605 Third Avenue, New York, NY 10158

Routledge is an imprint of the Taylor & Francis Group, an informa business

British Library Cataloguing-in-Publication Data
A catalogue record for this book is available from the British Library

ISBN: 9781032866833 (hbk)
ISBN: 9781032866840 (pbk)
ISBN: 9781003528685 (ebk)

DOI: 10.4324/9781003528685

Typeset in Times New Roman
by codeMantra

Contents

Figure

Introduction

In a friendly meeting, one of my friends shared with me a story about her nephew. She said that one morning, Artin, her two-and-a-half-year-old nephew, without giving notice, slipped off his shoes and went outside the house. When Artin's mother realized that Artin was missing at home, she searched everywhere for him. Unable to find any trace of him, she became worried and informed the entire family, friends, and acquaintances to help find Artin. The anxious and worried search continued for hours, while everyone was under pressure and stress, Artin returned home. When they asked him where he had been, he gave an answer that surprised everyone. Artin said, "I went to take a walk like Bernard. Bernard[1] the bear always goes out alone, so I went out alone too!"

Artin's behavior and the potential influence he might draw from an animated show could be a concern for parents, yet the situation is not necessarily chaotic or unsolvable. Artin had been watching television programs by himself, alone, without any active mediation by a knowledgeable adult between him and the television content.

To empower and protect children, the role of parents needs to shift from being mere supervisors to becoming facilitators and collaborators. This role aligns children and parents as a team and puts them side by side. Unlike in the past, where parents were seen as authority figures hovering over their children, in this role, parents are positioned alongside their children, acting as guides and companions in their media encounters. This activity results in strengthening the child's critical thinking. Amidst the multitude of messages presented in this world, the only solution is to empower children to analyze information critically. This can be achieved through the transformation of parents' role from supervisors to facilitators and collaborators.

In this book, my main aim is to guide parents on the critical role they play in mediating their children's media consumption. But before diving into that, let's step back a bit and explore the history of academic studies in media and children. My objective is to provide you with an understanding of media influence and the importance of active mediation.

DOI: 10.4324/9781003528685-1

In recent years, the presence of media and communication technologies in children's lives has instilled fear in many parents, a fear that can be attributed to various factors. I will explain the origins of this fear and how we can adopt a more positive perspective to help you understand both the tools and their applications needed to become a better facilitator [and collaborator] for your children. Consequently, we can assist children in navigating and growing in this media-saturated world while remaining safe and creative, and developing critical thinking skills. Through reading my book, you will come to realize that none of the perspectives regarding media is self-evident or absolute, and there are various ways to approach media and its functions.

The story goes that there has always been a defensive approach whenever any type of new technology emerges. This behavior is not exclusive to a specific society but is inherent to human nature. History shows that humans have always been fearful of new things that have the potential to disrupt the prevailing order. This fear has been directed toward things that may be difficult for us to believe. For instance, in the 18th century, reading novels was taboo, often met with negative reactions and deemed an undesirable act. This negative reaction stemmed from a kind of moral apprehension, originating from the observation of readers' enthusiasm for the imagination that they perceived as threatening to upend societal values (Vogrinčič, 2008).

Nevertheless, the story of resistance against communication technologies is interesting, and its basis can be found in the assumptions we hold about humans, their agency, and capabilities. Our reaction to the new conditions created by emerging communication technologies can be traced back to two underlying assumptions and the choice between them: one, assuming humans as strong beings with the ability to think independently, and the other perceiving humans as vulnerable creatures easily influenced and lacking independent thinking power. Each of these assumptions demands a different approach when confronted with new technologies. Based on this very point, one can explain a society's reaction toward media and communication technologies.

The initial body of academic literature concerning media and communication technologies often portrays a sense of fear and perceived danger associated with them, particularly concerning children and adolescents. According to this initial literature, it is commonly advised to parents to restrict their children from using these tools, citing various potential harms such as addiction, attention and concentration disorders, depression, aggression, anxiety, and many more, as consequences of their use. Since this perspective is also prevalent among parents themselves, they often embrace and enforce it when regulating their children's utilization of media and communication technologies. While newer research on media and emerging communication technologies may offer different perspectives, altering the initial impression created by earlier studies in this field can be challenging.

In fact, the repeated warnings from psychologists about the use of tablets, mobile phones, computer games, and similar technologies have fueled a growing opposition against these tools. Anxious parents often perceive a child engaged in activities such as computer gaming as a "lost child." These warnings have instilled such fear in parents that they are more inclined toward eliminating technology altogether rather than making an effort to understand the appropriate role of these technologies, similar to any other tools, in their own lives and the lives of their children. Many concerned parents approach me and express their worries, mentioning that their 11- or 12-year-old child is chatting online or that their 6-year-old is demanding a tablet from them. They are often seeking guidance on a solution to rescue their child from what they perceive as a threat.

Despite the criticism of moral panic around media and communication technologies, the main flaw in this perspective is that it evaluates media based only on its form and technology, ignoring the actual content. This perspective traces back to the initial ideas of Marshall McLuhan, who believed that "the medium is the message," implying that the form and shape of media have an impact on individuals regardless of the content. He classified media into two types, hot and cool, based on their form, each capable of eliciting different levels of audience participation. Hot media are those that induce less audience participation. They are linear, sequential, and non-participatory, delivering ready-made information to the audience, such as radio and film. However, cool media are nonlinear and participatory, engaging the audience more actively, such as books and telephones (Merchand, 1998).

The tendency to evaluate the influence and function of media solely based on its form and shape is clear from McLuhan's perspective. This viewpoint, originating from the earliest theories on media, has led to a marginalization of content and messages from the outset, resulting in less contemplation on their role and significance. The types of questions parents often ask are also typically influenced by this perspective. For example, they inquire, "Does television have an impact on children?" This question solely considers the technological and formal aspects of television, making it a flawed inquiry. Television encompasses various programs, and evaluating its impact requires assessing each content separately. For instance, a TV series undoubtedly has a different impact on children compared to a puppet show. However, parents cannot be blamed in this regard. If we review past scientific literature on media and children, you will see that this exact question was often posed as the central research inquiry in academic investigations.

In addition to television, these concerns also exist regarding new communication devices, and the same kind of question is being asked again. For example, they ask, "What is the impact of tablets and mobile phones on children?" This question also arises from incorrect assumptions. We cannot simply explain the impact of a tool that carries messages based solely on its form.

Certainly, technologies can have various functionalities. But do we go to the kitchen every morning, use knives, and draw lines everywhere? Do we place a vacuum cleaner in the refrigerator or sometimes camp into the fridge? If your answer is yes, then close this book right now and don't continue reading because this book is not for you. But if your answer is no, then you agree with me that it is now our creativity skill and resourcefulness to give specific positions to technologies like mobile phones, tablets, laptops, and so on. Engaging in a war with these technologies and dismissing the main problem don't help us, and the more we try, the more they will prevail. For these technologies to be able to be used in a more desirable way for the growth and development of our children and their well-being [and critical thinking skills], we must make peace with them as tools and learn to work with them in partnership. We should not allow them to control our behavior and mind. It is better to let go of these mental clichés about new tools and emphasize the positive applications of new communication technologies, rather than considering their use completely futile and negative. Opposing them is like going to battle with a wooden sword.

If you have contemplated the discussion, I've brought up so far, you will agree that I am talking about the ability of humans – humans who determine the functionality of every tool in their lives, humans who are knowledgeable and not under subjugation, humans who have agency and can define their relationship with tools, and overall, humans who are active, not passive. In this context, children also possess these very characteristics in varying degrees, with growth over time. Therefore, what I want to share with you in this book undoubtedly stems from the perspective of looking at humans as beings capable of unique power. This kind of perspective, which is equipped with a unique capability called "metacognition," shapes my approach in this book in dealing with technologies and communication tools. It is targeted at individuals who can reflect on their own habits, beliefs, attitudes, and selfhood in a thoughtful manner, as well as critically evaluate and improve their relationship with media and communication technologies. Based on this perspective, I initially place hope in the power of humans, and then, relying on this power, I provide strategies for confronting the new circumstances we are in.

Media and Communication Technologies Align with Human Needs

Often, along with the warnings given about the use of internet and communication technologies, we forget that the use of digital platforms and tools originates from human needs that should be addressed – needs that cannot be suppressed or disregarded. What are these needs? "Jan Dewey" categorizes these needs and believes that education should revolve around addressing four fundamental needs:

1 Inquiry and exploration: This refers to the need to ask questions and discover their answers.
2 Creation: The need to build or create something.

3 Connection: The need to establish connections and share ideas with others, in order to engage in social interaction and become part of the social world.
4 Self-expression: The need to express oneself, including emotions, ideas, beliefs, and more (Hayes, 2007).

Let's review this categorization of needs and their connection with media and new communication technology once again. The invention and advancement of media and communication technologies have also been shaped to address these very needs, catering to human desires for self-expression, connection, inquiry, and creative responses. That is why they cannot be eliminated from human life, and it is not helpful to have a negative perspective on their use. A negative perspective means focusing on the potential harms and constantly providing recommendations on how to avoid those harms. However, a positive perspective means focusing on the capacities and capabilities of online space and communicational technologies, discussing the actions that should be taken to grow and thrive through their utilization.

Note

1 Bernard is a computer-animated television series produced by RG Animation Studios.

References

Hayes, W. (2007). *Progressive education movement: Is it still a factor in today's schools?* Lanham, MD: Rowman & Littlefield Education.

Merchand, P. (1998). *Marshall McLuhan: The medium and the messenger: A biography.* Cambridge: MIT Press.

Vogorinčić, A. (2008). *The novel-reading panic in 18th-century England: An outline of an early moral media panic.* Medijska Istrazivanja/Media Research, 14(2), 103–124. Zagreb: University of Zagreb.

1 Common Parental Questions

Carrying out the mentioned perspectives in the introduction, in the upcoming sections, I have provided answers to fundamental and commonly asked questions by parents—questions that stem from their initial concerns and are often the primary considerations they have regarding media and communication technologies.

Does the Media Influence Children?

The initial belief among researchers regarding the relationship between children and media assumed that media has an impact on children. In the research of these researchers, discussions on the effects of media on children often focused solely on the negative aspects. Some critics, based on limited or no empirical evidence, argued that exposure to television could lead to consequences such as reduced attention span, disinterest in school, or the transformation of children into passive viewers (Fish, quoted by Bryant & Oliver, 2009).

In general, the initial theories in the field of media effects emphasized a strong and powerful influence of media on mass audiences. Theories such as magic bullet theory or hypodermic needle model are examples of these theories. They argue that the message functions like a bullet or a needle that penetrates the audience's brain and injects the effect. Influenced by these theories, the perception of media's impact on children also emerged. However, within this context, the emphasis on the influence of media on children was greater due to the vulnerability of children and the perspective influenced by the theories of Jean-Jacques Rousseau, which viewed children as innocent and vulnerable (Valkenburg, 2011). In fact, the initial concerns about the influence of media on children were centered around the idea that media were eroding childhood and homogenizing adults and children. Figures such as Mirovitz and Postman were pioneers of this belief (Valkenburg, 2011). They implicitly believed in the powerful influence of television and its ability to homogenize childhood with adulthood.

DOI: 10.4324/9781003528685-2

The theorists of the Frankfurt School, two decades before figures like Postman and Mirovitz, also emphasized the negative influence of media as a product of the culture industry. According to Adorno and Horkheimer (2002), the function of the culture industry is standardization and mass production, erasing any form of distinction and conflict in the realm of thought and culture, leaving no impact other than conformity, adaptation, submission, and isolation. This approach aligns with the theories related to media effects that considered the audience as passive and attributed the main power to the media.

In this context, the first theory that specifically emerged regarding the influence of media on children was Albert Bandura's (1971), which formulated the theory of social learning influenced by the behaviorist school of thought in psychology. The underlying assumption of this theory is that children learn behavior through two pathways: one through direct experience and the other through observing the behaviors of others. The second method of learning, namely observing the behaviors of others, is applicable in the context of media, as Bandura believed that children modify or construct their own behavior by observing the behaviors of others (which can include the behaviors of characters in films). At that time, there was a strong belief regarding this type of influence, namely learning behavior through observation.

However, the development of the cognitive school of thought in psychology, led by Jean Piaget, posed a fundamental challenge to this theory. Bandura's theory disregarded internal mental processes and perceived media influence as significant and uniform. According to Piaget, children were not passive beings who passively absorbed influences from their environment, including the media. Piaget (1929) attempted to explain children's behavior through specific cognitive structures called schemata. In his view, children actively engage in the process of understanding the world and do not merely observe and imitate it; rather, they interpret it (Singer & Revensen, 1996).

Piaget believed that children benefit from schemata to understand the things they see, hear, smell, and feel. Schemata are interconnected networks of thoughts, concepts, or relationships that exist in individuals' memory, enabling them to absorb and comprehend new information. Children construct these schemata through interactions with their environment. A schema is a mental framework that a person employs to interpret what they see and hear. For example, a child develops schemata about how to behave, eat, play, identify dangerous things, understand the characteristics of animals, and essentially anything else. They classify information about different subjects in their minds and place new information within the relevant schema. Each schema represents a category. Schemata organize perceptions and behaviors, empowering individuals to perceive and adapt to their environment accordingly (Singer & Revensen, 1996).

Due to the fact that children's schemata change in accordance with their age, older and younger children respond very differently to the information they receive from the environment, including the media. Piaget's perspective significantly influenced research on children and media, as it shifted the focus of researchers in this field. Initially centered on children's behavior, researchers later turned their attention to their cognitive effects, placing greater emphasis on variables such as attention, comprehension, and memory (Valkenburg, 2011). Furthermore, more attention was given to individual differences in processing media content. For example, researchers focused on the cognitive stage of children and the role of this factor in their attention and emotional responses when exposed to media content (Valkenburg, 2011).

Consequently, research and beliefs gradually moved away from initial assumptions about the specific and consistent influence of media on children, taking into account the active child and their internal cognitive characteristics, entering a new phase. Bandura (1989), as one of the pioneering researchers in this field, later, modified his social learning theory to align with the cognitive changes in psychology and insights related to the active child. In Bandura's more modern model, he placed greater emphasis on cognitive processes and self-regulation in children. He no longer believed that media necessarily have an impact but acknowledged that the influence can vary depending on the characteristics of the media message, the child, and the environment. This assumption that the effects on children are conditional and selective is now a fundamental paradigm in the realm of research on media influence among psychologists and researchers (Valkenburg, 2011).

In parallel with the shift in the perception of children as passive individuals in the field of psychology, theories within the realm of communication studies were also influenced by research focused on the audience. In these theories, children were regarded as individuals with agency, will, and independence from adults, capable of actively constructing meanings beyond the content of media.

Given the abundance of studies in the field of children and media, it can be concluded that media do not have a direct, explicit, and predetermined impact on children. Instead, the internal, historical, and cultural characteristics of children, as well as the level of caregivers' mediation, are key variables in how they receive media content. These are the qualities that children have acquired through their communication and interaction with the world around them, an interaction that involves individuals in their immediate surroundings as intermediaries for understanding the world. This point can serve as a fundamental clue for understanding the influence of media on children.

In general, the influence of media on children can be explained by considering the role of the "Vygotskian" mediator interpreted by Robert Fisher (2005). Inspired by Vygotsky's (1986) concept of mediator, he states that the child's caregivers, as mediators, control the stimuli received by the child and assist them in constructing their own world structure using patterns similar to caregivers. They are cultural conveyors that shape the attitudes, perceptions, and behaviors of children. When parents tell a child that certain objects or actions are good or bad, right or wrong, important or unimportant, they transmit cultural values to the child. This process involves the child's understanding and interpretation of the world.

Can Media Play as a Mediator and Provider of Meaning for Children, Similar to Their Parents and Caregivers and Social Acquaintances?

The response to this question is conditionally positive. In the absence of mediators such as parents, teachers, or any other individuals who hold authority and serve as a source of knowledge for the child, the media may potentially assume the role of mediator in successful meaning-making. For instance, when a child is consistently exposed to violent messages in movies, if parents remain silent and show no reaction to these messages, and if they do not interpret negative behaviors as inhumane for the child, their silence or indifference can be perceived as an endorsement of the messages. Under such circumstances, the media may shape the child's understanding of violence, its application, and the circumstances surrounding its use.

What Is the Impact of Television on Children? Is This Question a Valid Inquiry?

In answering the previous question, I discussed the general history of research on the impact of media. In this section, I would like to briefly address a specific question that is embedded within the previous discussion but, due to its significance and concern among many parents, I will provide a more precise elaboration on it.

Is it a valid question to ask, "Does television have an impact on children?" Television is one of those tools that has garnered significant speculation regarding its negative impact on children. Psychologists have consistently warned about issues such as attention disorders, hyperactivity, television addiction, etc. In other words, there exists a negative bias against television, leading parents to focus more on how to use less television rather than effectively guiding their children on its proper usage. This mindset places them in a battlefield against television, where television is already the winner.

In this particular stance toward television, what receives the most attention is the technological aspect and its form, rather than its content. Some psychologists believe that excessive television viewing, regardless of its content, can lead to various disorders such as hyperactivity and attention deficits in children. While it is a mistake and misleading to address television separately from its content, attributing the occurrence of these disorders solely to television viewing is the most preliminary conclusion drawn from research conducted in this field. This perspective on television dates back to a time when it was newly introduced to societies and did not have specialized programs for children. Consequently, children watched programs alongside adults that contained explicit sexual, violent, and inappropriate content. During that period, researchers were attempting to understand the impact of television on children, with a greater focus on the technological influence of television, independent of its content.

These types of studies were conducted because the science of media research and its impact on the audience was still in its early stages. They utilized quantitative methods to measure the impact of television, for example, by measuring the amount of time children spent watching television and then assessing characteristics such as violence, concentration level, learning abilities, and so on in children. They would then examine the relationship between the amount of television viewing time and the children's characteristics.

However, today these studies lack sufficient credibility in the field of science because researchers have learned from experience that it is the way television is utilized, the content of television, and most importantly, the cognitive variables of children (such as memory, attention, schemas, concentration, and cognitive stage) that determine the impact and reception of television on children. Since television content is divided into various categories, instead of asking what impact television has on children, we should ask *what do children perceive from a particular program?*

When we inquire about the impact of television on children, we are solely focusing on the form and technological aspect of television, unintentionally overlooking its content. Therefore, by posing the right question, we can arrive at a more accurate answer. Additionally, the current methodology employed in studying the role of television programs is either qualitative or a combination of qualitative and quantitative approaches. Researchers utilize these methods by conducting interviews with children, observing their behavior, or analyzing the content of programs. Generally, they employ qualitative methods that delve deeper and consider broader dimensions of the role of media in a child's life.

Now, we can respond to the question regarding the impact of television as follows: It is conditionally possible that certain programs may influence certain children. However, it should be noted that the impact is not always negative, and a program can potentially assist in a child's development. Active mediation by more knowledgeable people around children can ensure that this positive impact takes place.

At What Age Can Children Start Watching Television?

Considering the abundant studies conducted on the use of screens, including television, it is recommended to avoid screen time by children under the age of 18 months, including watching movies due to various reasons. The following are some of the reasons that justify this recommendation.

Television images, due to their brightness and continuous movement across various frames, captivate the attention of children from infancy. Since television images are perceived by infants as shapeless and chaotic forms, the exploration of the impact of technological aspects of television on children becomes more important than the content itself. In other words, children do not comprehend the content and certainly do not see the images as we do because they have yet to develop visual patterns in their memory that would enable them to understand the images.

Imagine a one-year-old child seeing an image of a donkey in a farm on television. They are unable to discern the lines that form the donkey and perceive the entire image as disjointed lines lacking any connection. This is why we say that for infants, the visual dimension of television images, in terms of form and shape, is the sole important aspect, not the content. Children under 18 months of age neither understand what the television is saying nor comprehend the images. They do not possess sufficient knowledge and schema to understand what exists on television can be a representation of reality. They lack any pre-existing categorized knowledge to relate what they see on television to their experiences. Their brains are incapable of comprehending the meaning of what they see on the television screen, and it is around the age of 18 months to 2 years that they begin to understand that the symbols portrayed on the television screen correspond to what exists in the real world.

The brains of children under 18 months are wired to learn from interacting with the world around them. When a child watches television, they are devoid of any interaction with the environment around them, which means that while they are engrossed in television viewing, they are not engaged in experiencing, touching, or playing, and therefore, they are not actively learning. What children at this age need to learn more than anything else is to interact with the people around them.

A child grows and develops more through banging on a pot than watching television. Children under 18 months need to touch objects, shake them, throw them (Ardiel & Rankin, 2010), see the faces they love, and hear the voices of the people they adore in order to learn. Therefore, infants under 18 months do not gain any valuable skills from television because television lacks all these capabilities.

Studies indicate that watching television before the age of 18 months can have a negative impact on language development, reading skills, and short-term memory (Hill, 2016). Although there are some exceptions, such as storybook-style programs, which could help with language development in children (Linebarger & Walker, 2005), television images constantly change and captivate the child's interest, but they can never compel or encourage the child to interact with them. Children, especially those under 18 months, are in the process of trying to increase their attention span, and excessive television viewing can make this task difficult for them. As a result, these children often face difficulties in attention focusing by the age of 7. The American Academy of Pediatrics considers television viewing for children under 18 months harmful.

In general, children under the age of 2 learn primarily through firsthand experiences in the real world and interacting with it. Every minute spent on visual media is a moment when your child is NOT exploring the world and NOT engaging their five senses which are crucial in their developmental process.

Watching television for children over 18 months of age differs significantly from children under 18 months. The most notable difference is that children over 18 months gradually develop the ability to learn and comprehend certain television programs. Around the age of 2, the child's brain undergoes significant changes, and the content of television becomes more important than its technological aspect. Children over 18 months, based on their experiences in the short span of their lives and the changes in their brain structure, can relate television images to the limited knowledge they have acquired.

Given the importance of content for children at this age and considering the interactive dimension in children's learning, it is necessary to categorize television contents into two types: interactive and non-interactive, in order to elucidate the relationship between children and television. Research indicates that interactive programs (i.e., programs that elicit responses from children, such as puppet shows that ask children questions) can teach children skills in writing, mathematics, problem-solving, or social behavior. These types of programs are commonly known as educational television and are designed in a way that encourages children's participation according to their age.

However, in general, to understand the relationship between media and children regarding interactive and non-interactive programs, an important point must be considered: children require a significant amount of categorized knowledge to comprehend what they see on television, which shapes their schemata over time. Therefore, what children understand from television largely depends on the content. Alongside the type of content, what matters in this context is how caregivers mediate the content for the child. Consequently, it can be concluded that children are allowed to watch television from the age of 2 onwards, and under specific conditions, television can contribute to the development of skills in children above the age of 2.

What Is Dependency on TV?

In the latest edition of the Diagnostic and Statistical Manual of Mental Disorders (DSM-5), television addiction is not recognized as a specific disorder. The DSM, which stands for the Diagnostic and Statistical Manual of Mental Disorders, serves as a standardized guide for classifying mental disorders and is developed by the American Psychological Association. The diagnostic criteria for classification of disorders and the inclusion of new disorders are based on scientific research. In the latest edition, a disorder specifically television addiction has not been identified. However, research suggests that dependency on television exhibits signs similar to addiction. Furthermore, one of the concerns within the realm of television and children is excessive television viewing by children.

Due to the significantly greater appeal of storytelling to children compared to adults, children are more prone to manifesting signs of television dependency. However, television images, due to their lack of complexity and continuous visual stimulation, do not require much concentration. Since focusing can be challenging for children and they find it difficult to concentrate easily, they engage in television viewing with greater comfort and without much difficulty. This interest in television viewing may escalate to the extent that they derive pleasure only from watching television and lose interest in other activities. This type of television dependency is commonly referred to as television addiction, but I prefer to cautiously label it as television dependency. The signs of this dependency include:

- The child engages solely in watching television instead of engaging in activities that are essential for their growth, such as playing with peers.
- They prefer to distance themselves from people around them and spend their time with television.
- When the television is turned off, the child becomes angry, sad, or restless.
- They have a long list of cartoons they must watch and easily become upset if they cannot watch them.
- Generally, they spend most of their time watching television and have no preference for any other form of recreation.

How Can We Actively Intervene to Help Children Dependent to TV?

Regardless of the child's age, it is important to have a conversation with them about this issue. Explain to them precisely why you are concerned and what are the potential harms of excessive television watching on their mind and body. Also, allow the child to express their opinion on whether they agree with the negative effects and let them share their reasons.

It is essential to persuade the child with logical reasons (rather than simply saying, "Mom or Dad doesn't want you to watch TV too much!"), to actively participate in breaking the habit of excessive television watching. Collaboratively find solutions and keep in mind that quitting this habit can be challenging for the child, so try to understand their perspective and motivate them by highlighting the detrimental impact of their behavior alongside other strategies.

Find alternative activities to engage the child. Often, these children admit to having no interest in any other form of entertainment. While this may be true, suggest that they try a few options; they will likely discover their interests again. Remind them that this lack of interest is temporary.

Gradually reduce the hours of television watching. Have planned activities for the child's leisure time and remember that your involvement is crucial for success in this endeavor.

Remember, enforce firm rules and limitations when it comes to media usage at home. Never use the television as a pacifier for your child and avoid making it their sole caregiver. Also, avoid assigning the most prominent spot in the house to the television, and refrain from placing a television set in the child's bedroom. Turn off the television when nobody is watching and review the content and rating of any movie before allowing the children to watch it.

It is important to approach this parenting strategy as a behavioral approach that fosters the child's internal motivation, rather than constantly forcing them to comply.

Attention Deficit Hyperactivity Disorder (ADHD) and Its Association with Television and Computer Games

Attention Deficit Hyperactivity Disorder (ADHD) is a neurodevelopmental disorder characterized by increased levels of hyperactivity, inattention, and impulsive behaviors, which are more pronounced and severe compared to other people who do not have this disorder (Furman, 2005). The primary difficulty experienced by children with ADHD is their inability to maintain and regulate their behavior (Nasa et al., 2018). As a result, they often struggle to act in a way that fits with what's happening around them. Their sleep and eating patterns are irregular, they appear to interfere in everything and require constant supervision. Emotionally, they lack stability, often exhibiting sudden laughter or crying, and their behavior is unpredictable or difficult to evaluate. They quickly move from one task to another and struggle to predict or evaluate the consequences of their actions.

They engage in risky activities, increasing their likelihood of getting injured (Ghirardi et al., 2019). They act before thinking, interrupting others before they finish speaking, throwing objects, and unintentionally harming others. They are also highly active and restless, as if they have a constant motor inside their bodies that compels them to be in constant motion. They are unable to sit still and often feel restless (Lukomski et al., 2021).

The concentration difficulties in these children are particularly evident in tasks that require sustained and focused mental activity. While they may not show significant differences in activities such as watching television, playing computer games, or engaging in enjoyable activities with other children, they exhibit noticeable differences in tasks that demand continuous mental activity and concentration, such as school assignments. It appears that their brains receive an excessive amount of environmental information, resulting in difficulties in selecting essential information, neglecting non-essential information.

Compliance with rules at home and school poses a challenge for them, requiring greater attention to adhere to regulations. They struggle with completing school assignments, focusing on academic tasks, following school rules, and establishing appropriate social relationships with classmates. They also struggle with long-term goal planning. In the following section, I have provided answers to common questions regarding the relationship between this disorder and children's use of technology.

Does Watching Animations (Due to the Continuous Frame Jumps) Reinforce This Disorder? And Can Computer Games Contribute to the Exacerbation of ADHD?

There is no strong evidence to suggest that television or computer games can cause or exacerbate ADHD (Nikkelen et al., 2014). In fact, it is possible that the heightened interest of hyperactive children in computer games and their increased engagement in gaming activities may lead to the misconception that computer games are the cause of their disorder. However, this conclusion could be misleading, as computer games are highly appealing to this group of children, and that is why they are more drawn to them.

What Types of Computer Games Are Beneficial for Children with This Disorder?

Computer games that require greater and longer focus and those where success is not solely based on quick reactions should be selected for them.

Why Are Computer Games and Animations Appealing to Children with ADHD?

Due to the significant difficulty that children with ADHD face in focusing, they find the rapid pace of television programs and video games particularly appealing. For example, if you watch the cartoon SpongeBob SquarePants, you will notice that not a second passes without something happening, and in most computer games, if you hesitate for a moment, you will lose. These games do not provide any opportunity for focusing on a specific situation and this characteristic makes them highly attractive to children with ADHD because they are not required to sustain their attention for long periods in a situation. "These games are constantly shifting focus, and there is instant gratification and reward" (Miller, n.d.). However, this does not mean that no computer games can benefit them. Research suggests that action-oriented computer games can improve players' ability to focus since during the game, they are compelled to concentrate on the gameplay itself, which enhances their concentration skills (Gong et al., 2017 and Campbell et al., 2023).

What Is the Primary Concern We Should Have Regarding This Type of Children?

Children with ADHD spend a significantly greater amount of time playing computer games, which means they allocate less time to other activities essential for their development. Since the main challenge for these children lies in social skills, excessive time spent on computer games can be more detrimental to them compared to other children. Therefore, the utmost effort should be focused on assisting them in establishing connections with other children and engaging in activities with them.

Addiction to Computer Game

Due to inherent attractiveness in computer games, they have the potential to induce addiction in children. The World Health Organization, in January 2018, announced that gaming disorder would be officially recognized as a disease, as experts in the field agree on the risks of addiction to these games. The organization stated that this disorder has been included in the 11th revision of the International Classification of Diseases (ICD-11), which was published in the summer of 2018. Furthermore, in the latest edition of the Diagnostic and Statistical Manual of Mental Disorders (DSM), gaming addiction has been proposed as a subject for further research to determine whether it should be classified as a diagnosable disorder or not.

In most cases, the root cause of the problem in children addicted to computer games must be sought within themselves. Research shows that children who often engage in computer games excessively may suffer from depression or some form of external environment-related distress (Tortolero et al., 2014). For this reason, they find solace in playing games in a world they can control, thus perceiving it not only as a behavioral issue but also as a mental health concern. When dealing with such children, it is important not to immediately resort to separating them from computer games as a first solution (as our initial instincts may lead us astray). Instead, the focus should be on identifying the underlying issue within the child.

All in all, remember that in addition to finding suitable computer games for your child, you should also limit their playing time. Even if the game involves physical movement, it is important to recognize that physical games played outside the home, interacting with friends and family, engaging in arts and crafts, and exploring other types of games are essential for a child's development.

Addiction to these games is similar to television dependency. The emotions a child experiences, the enthusiasm they have for playing, and the psychological states they go through are akin to being dependent on television. For this reason, when dealing with this condition and aiding in its resolution, it can be beneficial to revisit the section related to television dependency in this book.

Happiness Pattern in Computer Game

Computer games are designed in a way to make people dependent on them. They are specifically designed to exploit human happiness patterns and make players dependent. Understanding their strategies to make players dependent can help us better combat computer game addiction. It is important to have conversations with children about these strategies. In the following section, I have written about this pattern, inspired by the "Ben Shaher" happiness pattern (Janse, 2020), and I encourage you to discuss it with your child.

Individuals tend to experience happiness when they make progress in their work. It doesn't matter how significant the progress is; your brain is designed to generate feelings of happiness when you're making progress in your tasks. These emotions are produced to keep you engaged and interested in the work that is progressing.

The interesting point here is that the process of approaching a goal is more important than achieving the goal itself. In other words, individuals tend to be happier when they are making progress toward a goal rather than when they have achieved it. When they reach the goal, they may experience happiness for a few hours or even a few days, but it doesn't take long for those positive emotions to fade away as they become accustomed to the circumstance. However, the feeling of happiness arises as soon as you set another goal and make progress toward it.

The pattern of human happiness follows this structure: if you want to stay happy, you need to set goals and divide them into smaller objectives, striving to achieve those objectives. Even after reaching a goal, it is important to set another goal. One of the primary reasons for children's interest in computer games is precisely this aspect. Computer games provide them with a sense of satisfaction that often comes after achieving systematic progress. As they advance from one stage to another, they experience the joy of making progress toward a goal.

In fact, it is due to this very strategy that a new form of addiction has emerged in the modern era: addiction to computer games. Computer games are designed in such a way that they deliver small doses of happiness to the player. These games always present small goals in front of you and achieving them gives you a sense of accomplishment. Furthermore, immediately after winning a level, another goal appears, requiring you to leave it behind in order to progress to the next stage.

What Type of Films Are Suitable for a Child?

When it comes to choosing a suitable film for a child, there are several factors to consider. Parents usually assume that what they themselves understand from a film, children will also grasp to some extent. However, extensive research indicates that people's interpretations of a film can vary greatly. This reality is even more pronounced when it comes to children, as they still lack sufficient language skills to comprehend media language and have limited experience in understanding diverse concepts. In general, their world is not yet closely aligned with ours, and they do not possess a level of understanding comparable to adults when it comes to films. Their immediate environment is still unfamiliar to them. To make sense of the world, they construct their own schemata based on the limited information they have, which may be highly distorted and divergent from reality. In summary, it is important to always proceed with the assumption that children may not comprehend what adults perceive when watching a film.

The understanding of children's different perceptions of media has led to the categorization of films, software, books, animations, and all media products having age ratings in most countries. The content rating system of different types of media aims to classify them based on their suitability for the audience. This classification is done based on factors such as the type of display, themes like sexual relationships, depiction of violence or drugs, the use of vulgar language, or subjects that may not be suitable for children or adolescents. Most countries have forms of rating systems.

In some countries like Australia, government organizations are responsible for this classification. The weighting of specific factors in the decision-making process for classifications varies from one country to another. This means that a film may be classified differently in different countries.

For example, in a country like the United States, films with explicit sexual scenes may be restricted to certain age groups, while in countries like Germany or France, the same content may be deemed suitable for all ages. However, films with violent content in countries like the United States and Australia may be classified as appropriate for all ages, whereas in countries like France and Germany, this may not be the case.

Various countries classify films using specific terms. For example, G or General signifies that the film is suitable for all ages. PG or Parental Guidance suggests that the film is suitable for children under 15 but should be watched with an adult. And 18+ indicates that the film is suitable for individuals above the age of 18 and older. For instance, SpongeBob SquarePants has been classified as suitable for ages 6 and above. This classification considers the characteristics of the animation as well as the developmental traits of children under the age of 6. For example, children under 6 may not have sufficient cognitive capacity to comprehend the fast-paced, abundant visual elements and dialogue-rich nature of this animation. Consequently, watching this animation may lead to challenges in their ability to focus, as they are at an age when their minds are highly playful and concentrating can be difficult. This film does not contribute to enhancing their focusing skills.

When selecting a film for children, there are a few points to keep in mind. First, you should understand the context in which the film is made, what its story is about, and what concepts it conveys. Second, consider whether those concepts are understandable for children. Can a child comprehend the plot and the message of the film? To do this, you can engage with your child by asking questions after watching films to gradually understand how your child thinks about different films and their interpretations of the story. You can inquire about the film's plot, characters, and events. Through this process, you will gradually get to know your child better and actively play a role as a facilitator when needed.

Another important point is whether the chosen media product, which could be a film, animation, or computer game, encourages children to ask questions, utilize their imagination, and be actively engaged and creative. Watching a film is not necessarily a passive and motionless activity; movies can stimulate various questions in the viewer's mind, provoke curiosity, and design activities that can be pursued after the program ends. Therefore, always consider the potential impact of films and computer games when making choices.

The next question to ask is to what extent these programs have commercial and advertising goals. The primary objective of many media products is to generate income for certain commercials or similar businesses. We must always consider what product or idea the film is advertising and ultimately benefiting whom. Another important point is to pay attention to the prevalent themes and concerns of these programs. If the desired program is a series, watch a few initial episodes to understand the main topics. What positive and negative characteristics are depicted? Which behaviors and activities are rewarded, and which ones are punished? What does the program deem important, valuable, or desirable?

Another important point to consider is how the desired media product portrays gender and individual differences. If films convey a sense to children that they should view themselves as inferior in aspects such as race, ethnicity, physical abilities, gender, and other traits compared to the characters depicted in the media, it can diminish their self-esteem and sense of worth.

Pay attention to the emotional and psychological impact these programs have on children. It is important to note that children's emotional reactions are often different from those of adults. Certain elements of the program's storyline, such as a simple conflict between two characters or the endangerment of someone's life, may seem ordinary to us as adults, but these same conflicts can have profound effects on young children. Remember that children differ from one another; do not assume that just because you enjoyed a program during your own childhood, all children will watch it without any issues.

Why Do Children Watch a Film Multiple Times?

When I do research with children and ask them, for example, how many times they have watched a particular film, sometimes they may say they haven't watched it much. Then I ask them to tell me approximately how many times they have watched it, and they respond with figures like ten or eight times. For adults, this may seem like many viewings for a film, but for children, watching a film repeatedly is completely normal and is not considered a sign of dependence. The reason for this relates to the characteristics of children. Children do not yet have enough categorized information in their minds to process and classify the information from a film in just one viewing. With each viewing, they acquire new information from the film and categorize it in their minds. The information presented in the film is overwhelming for children, and they usually continue to rewatch it until they have processed all the information it contains.

From What Age Can Children Start Using Tablets and Mobile Phones?

It is typically from the age of 3 onwards that many children can become active users of media and benefit from educational content on electronic devices, provided that their use does not replace physical play or engagement with the outside world.

Susan Schwartz, a learning specialist at Child Mind Institute, explains that when a child under the age of 3 interacts with objects in the real world and engages in play with three-dimensional objects, their entire body is in motion, aligned with the act of playing with tangible objects (Martinelli, 2023). Consequently, tactile and visual information is transmitted to their brain, allowing them to fully interact and learn from the real world. However, when a child under the age of 3 is learning to use a mobile device or playing with an application, their entire body is not actively engaged in comprehending the spatial context (compared to when they interact with the real world). Therefore, parents seeking educational activities for children under the age of 3 should be aware that playing with toys such as building blocks provides more suitable and beneficial learning experiences compared to apps and videos designed for children in this age group.

What Is the Right Way for Children to Use Smartphones and Tablets?

Tools such as tablets, smartphones, and computers can be used both online and offline. These tools are user-centric, allowing children to choose how to use them. They can watch movies, play games, draw, write, access various websites, acquire information, find virtual friends, and more, both online and offline. Given the diversity of possible activities, working with these tools can be an extraordinary intellectual adventure for children. The advantage of these tools is that children can actively engage with them and, unlike other devices like television, they are not passive recipients. In fact, when a person is not fully engaged in an activity, instead of the individual controlling the activity, it is the possibility that the activity controls the individual.

Therefore, if we look at the new tools from an interactive perspective, we can educate our children to use these tools in various ways. The concept of interactivity in these tools means empowering the user and emphasizing their decision-making power, which essentially controls the machine. This is where we should shift our focus from asking "How much should children use these tools?" to asking "How should children use these tools?"

The use of communication tools like tablet and smartphone for children aged 3 and above does not hinder development, as they can be utilized to support children's growth. However, if their usage is not purposeful and regulated, they can be harmful. When it comes to children's use of mobile devices and tablets, instead of constantly focusing on behaviors that children "should not" exhibit in their media usage, we should concentrate on behaviors that they "should" have regarding the appropriate use of media and communication technologies.

In doing so, rather than focusing on negative behaviors of the child and imposing punishments for inappropriate media usage, it is preferable to concentrate on positive behaviors of the child and provide rewards and attention for them. Additionally, it is important to establish rules and structures that clearly teach the child what kind of positive uses they should have while using media and communicational technologies.

In this case, the child gradually adjusts their behavior in using media and communication technologies, and even when there is no external control, they do not change their approach. Being focused on negative behaviors and punishment may make you feel better, but it doesn't change the child's behavior. Instead of punishment, reinforce the positive behavior you want from the child until the negative behavior eventually diminishes (Kazdin, 2021),

Key points to consider for fostering healthy way of using tablet and mobile habits in children include:

1 Be a role model for your child.
2 When you are with your child, set aside laptops, mobile phones, and tablets.
3 Use technology in a rule-governed purposeful manner
4 Children listen to only 1% of what we tell them but observe and absorb almost all of our actions.
5 When your child under the age of 6 uses a computer or mobile device, ask them some questions. It is better to inquire about what they are doing on the computer, mobile phone, or tablet. Encourage them to think about what they see on the screen by asking questions such as: "How do you play the game?," "What happens when you press that button?," or "Which character is speaking?"
6 If your child asks for a tablet or mobile phone, and you intend to buy one for them, be sure to ask them exactly what they want to use it for. Remind them that these tools are designed to assist us in achieving our goals. Ask

them to convince you first of how the tablet or mobile phone will be useful to them. In the process, try to indirectly help them discover positive functions of these devices.

7 Conduct the conversation in a way that allows your child to persuade you. Now that you have set the goal, it is time to establish rules. The use of tablets should have a maximum duration and exceeding that limit should be considered a violation of the rules. Once you have reached an agreement on this matter, strive to enforce these rules strictly, as childhood is the best time to internalize the patterns of proper usage of these communication technologies.

If you constantly feel concerned when your child is using media and communication technologies, remember that you are not as powerless as it may seem, and you can have a positive impact on your child's behavior and growth. The most valuable assistance I can provide is emphasizing the importance of interaction in your child's learning and cognitive development. Nothing allows humans to grow as much as interaction does. One of the main learning for children is learning through interaction with humans. When a child interacts with a person, their brain activity is significantly more active.

However, if your child spends hours alone, endlessly scrolling through your mobile phone, it is completely justified to feel guilty. However, when you engage with each other using the mobile phone, asking questions, and having conversations, your child is actively learning, and there is no need to worry.

This is true for all forms of media. When you spend time with your child and actively watch television together, you gradually develop a common language with your child. This language expands over time, allowing you to gain a deeper understanding of concepts that are shared with your child. This shared language reduces tensions in your relationship with your child, both in the present and in the future. Therefore, try your best to interact with your child during their use of media and communication technologies.

It is essential to make children aware of the physical harm caused by uninterrupted staring at monitors, prolonged sitting, and continuous use of a mouse and keyboard without breaks. They must be taught proper sitting posture, the appropriate duration of computer usage, and overall, how to use computers and mobile devices from an early age. The instruction and education regarding these matters should be taken seriously, as the physical damage resulting from improper use of these tools is sometimes irreversible.

Is Video call Harmful for Children?

As I mentioned, children under the age of 3 are advised against using mobile phones and tablets. However, there is an exception to this rule, and that is video communication between children under 3 and their close relatives through platforms such as WhatsApp, Facebook, Skype, and similar applications. Using these tools for visual communication and interaction has a positive impact on a child's development. In 2016, the American Academy of Pediatrics revised its policy regarding children's exposure to communication technologies. The academy acknowledged that interactive learning and communication opportunities provided by communication technologies offer positive learning experiences and the establishment of relationships for children, which television is unable to provide. In fact, communication through video apps helps children gradually build their social connections. Although video calls cannot replace the benefits of spending time with a child in the real world, the positive impact of video communication can still be regarded as valuable.

Researchers have found that infants can comprehend whether a person they see on television, or a mobile device is interacting with them or not, starting at around six months of age. This means that they can form social or emotional relationships with individuals who are physically distant from them, especially if the chats are facilitated by an adult present with them (for example, having a father beside the child during a video chat and saying, "Grandma is talking to you," pointing to the screen with their hand, waving their hand, describing the video, etc.). Even if your child does not say anything, they are actively receiving visual and social cues and shaping their understanding of the individuals they are interacting with through video chats.

Emerging evidence shows that at 24 months of age, children can learn words from live video chatting with a responsive adult (Hill et al., 2016). Regarding the interactive characteristics of video chat, they learn more through it than educational programs on mobile devices, television, and other tools. This is because video chats allow the adult to respond in accordance with the child's actions, thus transforming the interaction into a reciprocal relationship.

Should We Stop Sharing Images of Children on Social Media?

The issue of sharing images of children online is highly challenging. We are still unaware of the potential harm and opportunities associated with it. Furthermore, children whose images are present online or whose parents utilize them for financial gain are often not old enough to share their own stories and provide a comprehensive understanding of the situation. In fact, the use of children's images can occur in two ways: first, parents or relatives may simply share their child's image to document moments with their audience, and second, children may be exploited for financial or other personal purposes.

To understand the advantages and disadvantages of sharing images of children by others on the internet, one solution is to wait until they grow up and then have conversations with them about their experiences and feelings. Another approach is to ask older individuals to put themselves in the shoes of children whose images have been shared and to discuss their emotions with us. I chose the second approach, and in order to gain a better understanding of this issue and assess its dimensions, I posed a thought-provoking question to my social media audiences.

My intention was not to conduct structured scientific research but rather to explore aspects that I might have never considered before. My question was as follows:

> Imagine that a photo of you as a child (under the age of 10) is shared on the internet by your parents, friends, or anyone else. In this photo, you are nose-picking, or you are crying with tears on your cheeks, wearing a diaper, or you are striking a funny pose. Can you tell me what kind of emotions would arise in you? Would it be discomfort, anger, indifference, a sense of amusement, or something else precisely?

Approximately 28 individuals responded to me, and their responses shed light on various factors to consider when drawing conclusions about the dos and don'ts of sharing photos of children. Age, gender, cultural background, and type personality were identified as factors that should be considered when sharing images. Among the participants, men expressed that it does not matter to them what photos of themselves are shared and they believe it would be "funny." All of them were above 20 years old and did not express any feelings of discomfort or embarrassment. However, most women stated that they do not like such images of themselves to be shared.

Their responses indicate that in order to decide whether we can share a photo of children, we need to consider the culture in which we live and ask ourselves how it would make our child feel if they saw the photo when they grow up. However, we should also consider that our child will likely be upset if they see the image as a teenager. When we share a photo of a child, it remains on the internet. As the child grows older and becomes an adolescent, their childhood photo still exists online. If they see this photo during their teenage years, it may be distressing for them, even though they may find it cute and appealing at a later age. It will undoubtedly be painful for them during a certain period. For example, if a seven-year-old child sees a nude photo of themselves from when they were four years old, it will cause distress because they don't perceive their four-year-old self as being from a long time ago.

Sometimes parents may obtain permission from their child at any age to justify sharing a seemingly cute photo of them. However, since a child goes through stages of development, each with unique personality and cognitive characteristics, they may have different feelings about displaying that photo to others at each stage. Additionally, they lack the ability to fully comprehend the long-term impact of that photo on their life. That is why sharing images based on the justification of having the child's consent is not acceptable and essentially it is meaningless. Therefore, when sharing photos of children, be cautious not to publish anything that would be embarrassing in your culture, as it is our responsibility to protect children.

Before sharing photos of children, ask yourself the following questions:

- Will it enhance the child's skills or development?
- Does the child actually want their photo to be shared?
- Will it not undermine their self-confidence?
- Will concerns about not receiving enough Likes bother them?
- Does the child perceive a lack of Likes as a sign of disapproval and become upset?
- Could the published photos potentially embarrass them in the future?

References

Ardiel, E. L., & Rankin, C. H. (2010). The importance of touch in development. *Paediatr Child Health*, 15(3), 153–156. https://doi.org/10.1093/pch/15.3.153. PMID: 21358895; PMCID: PMC2865952.

Bandura, A. (1971). *Social learning theory*. New York: General Learning Press.

Bandura, A. (1989). Social cognitive theory. In R. Vasta (Ed.), *Annals of child development. Vol. 6. Six theories of child development* (pp. 1–60). Greenwich, CT: JAI Press.

Bryant, J., & Oliver, M. (2009). *Media effects advances in theory and research*. London: Routledge.

Campbell, M. J., Cregan, S. C., Joyce, J. M., Kowal, M., & Toth, A. J. (2023). Comparing the cognitive performance of action video game players and age-matched controls following a cognitively fatiguing task: A Stage 2 registered report. *British Journal of Psychology*, 115(3), 363–385. https://doi.org/10.1111/bjop.12692

Fisher, R. (2005). *Teaching children to think*. Second Edition. United Kingdom: Nelson Stanley Thornes.

Furman, L. (2005). What is attention-deficit hyperactivity disorder (ADHD)? *Journal of Child Neurology*, 20(12), 994–1002. https://doi.org/10.1177/08830738050200121301

Ghirardi, L., Chen, Q., Chang, Z., Kuja-Halkola, R., Skoglund, C., Quinn, P. D.,…, & Larsson, H. (2019). Use of medication for attention-deficit/hyperactivity disorder and risk of unintentional injuries in children and adolescents with co-occurring neurodevelopmental disorders. *Journal of Child Psychology and Psychiatry*, 61(2), 140–147. https://doi.org/10.1111/jcpp.13136

Gong, D., Ma, W., Gong, J., He, H., Dong, L., Zhang, D., Li, J., Luo, C., & Yao, D. (2017). Action video game experience related to altered large-scale white matter networks. *Neural Plasticity*, 2017, Article ID 7543686. https://doi.org/10.1155/2017/7543686

Hill, D. (2016). *Why to avoid TV for infants & toddlers*. American Academy of Pediatrics. Retrieved May 2024, from https://shorturl.at/inxAD

Hill, D. et al. (2016). Media and young minds. *Pediatrics*, 138(5), e20162591. https://doi.org/10.1542/peds.2016-2591

Horkheimer, M., & Adorno, T. W. (2002). *Dialectic of enlightenment: Philosophical fragments* (G. Schmid Noerr, Ed.; E. Jephcott, Trans.). Stanford University Press. Stanford, CA. (Original work published 1947)

Janse, B. (2020). *Tal Ben-Shahar's happiness model.* Retrieved April 2023, from Toolshero https://www.toolshero.com/psychology/happiness-model/

Kazdin, A. E. (2021). The Kazdin method for developing and changing behavior of children and adolescents. *International Journal of Mental Health Promotion*, 23(4), 429–442. https://doi.org/10.32604/IJMHP.2021.019135

Linebarger, D. L. and Walker, D. (2005). Infants' and toddlers' television viewing and language outcomes. *American Behavioral Scientist*, 48(5), 624–645. https://doi.org/10.1177/0002764204271505

Lukomski, M., Caruso, D., Thompson, K. M., & Natale, M. D. (2021). A program to improve the assessment of a child for attention deficit hyperactivity disorder. *Journal of Child and Adolescent Psychiatric Nursing*, 35(2), 164–170. https://doi.org/10.1111/jcap.12361

Martinelli, K. (2023). *Can screen time be educational for toddlers?* Childmind Institute. Retrieved May 2024, from https://childmind.org/article/value-screen-time-toddlers-preschoolers/

Miller, K. (n.d). *Do Video games cause ADHD*? Childmind Institute. Retrieved May 2024, from https://shorturl.at/iryzQ

Nasa, A. F., Pudjiati, S. R. R., & Tjakrawiralaksana, M. A. (2018). Application of a shaping technique to increase on-task behavior duration in children with ADHD. *Proceedings of the 1st International Conference on Intervention and Applied Psychology* (ICIAP 2017). https://doi.org/10.2991/iciap-17.2018.13

Nikkelen, S. W. C., Valkenburg, P. M., Huizinga, M., & Bushman, B. J. (2014). Media use and adhd-related behaviors in children and adolescents: A meta-analysis. *Developmental Psychology*, 50(9), 2228–2241. https://doi.org/10.1037/a0037318

Piaget. J (1929). *The child's conception of the world.* London. Routledge & L Paul

Singer, D. G., & Revenson, T. A. (1996). *A Piaget primer: How a child thinks* (Rev. ed.). New York. Plume.

Tortolero, S. R., Peskin, M. F., Baumler, E. R., Cuccaro, P. M., Elliott, M. N., Davies, S. L., Lewis, T. H., Banspach, S. W., Kanouse, D. E., & Schuster, M. A. (2014). Daily violent video game playing and depression in preadolescent youth. *Cyberpsychology, Behavior, and Social Networking*, 2014 Sep; 17(9), 609–615. https://doi.org/10.1089/cyber.2014.0091. Epub. PMID: 25007237; PMCID: PMC4227415.

Valkenburg, P. (2011). *Children's responses to the screen.* London: Lowrence Erlboum Associates Piblisher.

Vygotsky, L. S. (1986). *Thought and language.* Edited and translated by Alex Kozulin. Cambridge: MIT Press.

World Health Organization (2018). *Gaming disorder.* Retrieved from https://www.who.int/standards/classifications/frequently-asked-questions/gaming-disorder

2 Violence in Media and Its Impact on Children

A Critical Perspective on Media Violence Theories

The inquiry into the impact of media violence on children typically is one of the main parents' questions. Given its significance as a prevalent concern within society, extensive research has been conducted in this field. As a result of these investigations, nearly six main theories have been proposed by researchers outlining the influence of media violence. All of these theories are presented in the book 'Children's Responses to the Screen: A Media Psychological Approach' by Patti M. Valkenburg (2011). I have briefly explained them along with a critical perspective on them.

Social Learning Theory

This theory represents the earliest perspective on the influence of media on its audience, including children and adolescents. According to this theory, behavioral violence can be learned through the observation of aggressive behaviors by others. In this theory, children do not receive direct rewards or punishments for violence while watching a film, but they associate violence with its consequences through exposure to it in their environment (including media). As a result, they may either replicate or avoid such behaviors.

For example, if a child sees someone being punished for violent behavior on television, they are less likely to repeat that behavior. However, if they witness violence being rewarded or go unpunished, they may be more inclined to replicate violent behavior in the real world.

The main drawback of this theory is its failure to consider the internal factors within individuals and their environmental conditions that contribute to violent behavior. It provides a superficial understanding of this process. Unfortunately, despite its numerous limitations, this theory has remained the most widely accepted among society.

DOI: 10.4324/9781003528685-3

Catharsis Theory

Contrary to prevailing theories on violence, Catharsis theory asserts that media violence has a positive impact on children. However, how is this possible? Proponents of Catharsis theory acknowledge that exposure to violent imagery can awaken aggressive emotions in children, but these emotions are discharged and emptied when they engage in viewing violence in the media.

They claim that children have innate aggressive tendencies, but by watching violent movies, they can release these feelings, leading to decreased aggression and a more peaceful state afterward.

It is important to note that this theory has not been proven through scientific research; however, it does have supporters within the realms of cinema and film studies. Advocates of this theory defend it based on psychoanalytic theories. Nonetheless, due to the lack of empirical evidence supporting the theory cannot be regarded as highly credible.

Desensitization Theory

According to this theory, if children are consistently exposed to violent films and imagery, their sensitivity toward media violence gradually decreases in real-life situations. The core premise of the desensitization theory is that repeated exposure and continuous immersion in media violence lead to these effects.

This repetition of exposing to violent films and imagery causes individuals to become accustomed to inhumane behaviors, resulting in not only experiencing less distress from violence depicted in films but also exhibiting more lenient moral judgments toward violence in media and real-life contexts, making it easier for them to justify violent acts.

The theory suggests that negative emotions in children, such as fear and anxiety, act as inhibitory factors for engaging in violence in real life. However, if children are consistently exposed to media violence, these emotions are diminished, increasing the likelihood of their involvement in aggressive activities.

This theory is not limited to children alone, but rather addresses the overall impact of media violence on individuals. I have three scenarios to critically examine this theory. Let's consider three scenarios:

- Scenario one: A police officer punches a dangerous person in the face to apprehend him.
- Scenario two: A thief punches an unarmed elderly person in the face to steal her belongings.
- Scenario three: The protagonist of a story punches an innocent man in the face for reasons aligned with human values, in order to achieve a goal.

The desensitization theory categorizes all these actions under the label of violence. However, do you think witnessing these three scenarios have the same effect on a child's mindset, behaviors, and judgments regarding violence?

Schema Theory

To describe this theory, we first need to briefly review the concept of schemas. Schemas represent our knowledge about the structure and organization of everyday life activities that we typically engage in. For example, knowledge about how people eat lunch, take a shower, or react when they get angry. According to this theory, media plays a role in constructing a portion of these schemas in a child's mind.

For instance, regarding violence, when a child watches a film in which an angry character yells and shouts, they may develop a schema in their mind that associates such behavior with expressing anger. Alternatively, the response of a character in a film to someone else's anger might also shape a schema in the child's mind.

This theory suggests that if children are repeatedly exposed to violent media scenes, there is a risk that their schemas become more aggressive and influence their future behavior. According to this theory, media is not the cause of violence in children, but it can teach them how to behave during moments of anger and frustration. However, a limitation of this theory is that it does not require a prerequisite for the media to construct schemas in a child's mind.

The prerequisite is that if parents do not actively intervene and express their dissatisfaction with violent behaviors directly or indirectly when witnessing violent scenes (if the displayed behavior is repeated), may turn into a schema in the child's mind.

The Arousal Theory

This theory posits that violent films arouse children. Arousal is a physical response to a film that results in increased breathing, elevated heart rate, increased blood pressure, excessive sweating, and similar reactions. According to this theory, when violence is combined with excessive movement, loud music, and a fast-paced narrative, the likelihood of arousal increases.

The Arousal Theory states that this type of influence does not quickly disappear after watching a film and can manifest itself in children's play and interactions with other children. According to this theory, media products that keep children in an excited state, even if they are not explicitly violent, are more likely to lead to violent behavior compared to products that are explicitly violent but do not keep children in an excited state.

The main limitation of this theory is that it only reduces the outcome of violence to physical arousal and does not address the impact of exposure to violent portrayals on children's understanding and perception of violence. In fact, from this perspective, a violent film has a blind effect that does not target anything specific but only induces physical arousal, resulting in increased excitement in children's behavior, which can lead to violence. Furthermore, it does not differentiate between films in terms of the type of violence and the concept of violence portrayed in them considering any film that contains violence to have these effects.

Priming Theory

This theory views human memory as a collection of interconnected networks. Each of these networks consists of related units that represent thoughts, emotions, behavioral tendencies, etc. According to this theory, an external stimulus (e.g., violence in a film) activates one or more units in memory, which can simultaneously activate related semantic units.

Based on this premise, violence in the media can increase the accessibility of aggressive semantic units. This accessibility can be temporary or continuous. When aggressive units are activated by violent stimuli, the likelihood of these specific units being used continuously for the perception and interpretation of violence in the media and the external environment increases.

To clarify it more, here is a description of an experiment: In an experiment, 40 students were studied. Twenty of them were exposed to a violent film, while the other half watched a non-violent film. At the end of the film, each participant was presented with 48 words. Half of these words were real English words, and the other half were meaningless words.

The participants were asked to press key 1 if they thought the word was an English word and key 2 if they thought it was not an English word. Unbeknownst to the participants, half of the selected words had aggressive meanings, while the other half did not.

The results showed that children who were exposed to the violent film had faster reactions when they heard violent words compared to children who had not seen the violent film. According to this experiment, this faster reaction can be attributed to priming. The violent film led to temporary increased accessibility to aggressive semantic units in their memory, resulting in a quicker response in children who had watched the violent film.

To enhance your understanding, I provide a clear example. A child who has watched a violent film may comprehend aggressive messages more quickly or interpret different situations as being more violent. Therefore, they exhibit a reaction that they have previously learned in response to violence, which could be either a fight-or-flight response. This theory does not claim that media causes violence; rather, it suggests that media primes and can reinforce conditions conducive to violence.

Mitigating the Potential Impact of Media Violence on Children

Despite the criticisms they receive, all these theories can be partially valid to some extent, depending on different circumstances and contexts. However, what can we do in order to mitigate the potential impact on children? Generally, researchers in the field of children and media believe that the effects of media on children are highly contingent on how they engage with media content. For example, violence in media affects children when:

- The child enjoys from that violence.
- The child identifies with the aggressive character in the film.
- The displayed violence is perceived as real by the child.

Active parental mediation is the most effective strategy for neutralizing the impact of violent content in the media and transforming this threat into an opportunity. Therefore, when watching a film containing violent scenes, it is recommended that parents:

- Clearly express their dissatisfaction with the violent scenes.
- Emphasize the fictional nature of media productions and their lack of realism.
- Encourage their child to empathize with the victim by fostering a sense of empathy.

By taking these actions, you can potentially convert the negative influence of the media into a positive one and foster the growth of empathy in your child.

Refernce

Valkenburg, P. (2011). *Children's responses to the screen*. London: Lowrence Erlboum Associates Piblisher.

3 Applying Media and Communication Technology for Children's Skills Improvement

Enhancing Children's Language Intelligence through Media

Thinking requires knowledge of words and concepts. The more vocabulary we possess, the easier and better we can think. However, cognitive development is intricately linked to the expansion of the conceptual framework. In other words, the more words children know, the greater their cognitive skill improves. One effective method of learning numerous concepts to children is through exposure to news media. Each news piece contains a multitude of words that can contribute to a child's conceptual and cognitive development.

When listening to news, such as scientific, cultural, or sport news, encourage your child to describe some of the news stories they have heard and, if they are willing, express their opinions about those events. This exercise aids in their cognitive skill and vocabulary development.

Utilizing Computer Games to Enhance Children's Skills

Children exhibit a great deal of interest in computer games, and it is impractical to completely restrict them from playing. Therefore, I would like to provide you with some suggestions to enable you to make the most of these computer games in fostering children's skill development.

Sometimes, it is better to allow children to teach us. When your child is engaged in playing with a mobile device or a computer, take the opportunity to inquire about the game and ask them to teach you about its various stages or what actions need to be taken to progress. Allow them to explain it to you according to their own understanding. Listen attentively to their explanations and ask open-ended questions. An open-ended question is one that does not have a short and definitive answer, and different individuals may have different perspectives on it. Give them the chance to demonstrate what they have accomplished in the game and describe it to you from their own perspective. For example, you can ask, "What are you trying to achieve? What happens if you press that button?" Since every game generally has a storyline, this

DOI: 10.4324/9781003528685-4

approach helps your child practice creative storytelling skills. Moreover, older children can enhance their problem-solving skills through this method.

Inquire your child about what they have discovered at each stage of the game. Determine what your child has learned from play. It may be necessary to ask them questions that are guiding, such as:

- What did you do in this new stage?
- Have you done this before?
- What was the most exciting part of the game for you?
- Did you learn any new words or concepts while playing?
- What should you do to make similar things happen?

Keep in mind that computer games should not replace physical activities for children. It is crucial that you can connect children's experiences in computer games to their real-world experiences! But how can you do that? Observing and playing with children provides you with information that you can utilize in this way. For example, ask:

- Can you tell me how the snakes were moving in that game you played?
- Do you remember what they were eating?
- How many coins/people/animals are there here (in the computer game)? Let's count.

Offline Games

It is essential for children to engage in unstructured and free play, where they can make decisions about what to do, how to do it, and play not just for the sake of reaching the next level (as in computer games) or learning a specific skill, but for the enjoyment of the play itself.

Children should derive pleasure from the experience of creating and breaking their own game rules. Offline games often possess these characteristics, so their value should not be underestimated. Such games help children to:

- Have this opportunity to chart their own path instead of constantly having their path dictated by the game.
- Enhance their creativity.
- Continuously experience decision-making.
- Practice collaboration and interaction with others.
- Learn to be a leader.

Characteristics of Computer Games Beneficial for Children Under 6

To determine which games are beneficial for children under the age of 6, Verenikina et al. (2010) has done a comprehensive review on the academic literature on characteristics of computer games that promote young children's development. She has listed following characteristics:

- The game is intrinsically fun and is not limited in scope to 'teaching' particular skills.
- It allows play for the sake of play—reaching goals is less important.
- It relates to daily life—sounds and objects from daily life, and other things that the child can recognize.
- The game can be incorporated into children's imaginative play.
- It is discovery oriented.
- It allows children choices in selection and timing of activities.
- The game allows the manipulation of symbols and images on the computer screen.
- It provides the facility to engage collaboratively with the program rather than exclusively single player.
- It provides visible transformations.
- The game enables increasing complexity.
- It provides spoken directions (as children may not be old enough to read), or provides advice that children need assistance from more experienced players.
- It employs an uncluttered screen design with simple background, coloring, and graphics.

Overall, the game should have multiple levels, gradually increasing in difficulty, allowing the child to match their skills with the game's level. The ability for a child to adjust their skills to the game's difficulty level helps them initiate an exploratory and unpredictable learning process. As they progress further, they can encounter more challenging levels along the way.

The game should grant them the opportunity to choose. Select games that allow your child to make choices based on their preferences and interests, rather than having everything predetermined by the software. The freedom to choose colors or characters in the settings, as well as providing options and alternatives throughout the game, nurtures a sense of independence and a feeling of control in your child.

Children aged 3 and above usually have a peculiar interest in animal recognition and imitating their sounds. Therefore, games that incorporate such content and respond to their interest can be beneficial. Additionally, games that contribute to the development of emotional intelligence skills and the understanding of emotions in children are highly valuable. Numerous games focus on this aspect, teaching emotions in an engaging and musical manner.

Check the age ratings of the games and read reviews written about those games. There are websites that classifies and provides descriptions for all computer and video games, helping parents understand the type of content in the game. After you have read some reviews with your child and discussed them, you can decide whether to try the game.

Also, remember that the game should not contain stereotypical representations, cultural biases, or violence. Certain activities within the game might inadvertently incorporate cultural or gender biases. For example, negative character voices may be associated with a specific accent. Therefore, it is important to be mindful of these stereotypical representations, as children under the age of 6 are highly susceptible to internalizing them.

The potential for involving other individuals in the game is an excellent characteristic of a quality game. Having the option to play with others provides your child with an opportunity to talk about learning and exploration. This conversation can be an exceptional way to understand what your child is experiencing. You might be surprised by seeing your child encountering something entirely different from you in the game.

Fostering Creativity through Media and Communication Technologies

One of the concerns surrounding media and communication technologies is that they may diminish creativity skills in individuals, including children. Given that children are in a phase where their creativity skills are developing, this concern becomes even more pronounced. In the following sections, I provided you with some solutions to help enhance your child's creativity using these very media and communication technologies.

Utilizing Films and Animation to Enhance Children's Creativity

According to the prominent learning theorist Vygotsky (2004), creativity is not something that simply inspires us but is rather a result of multiple experiences and their combination. To better understand Vygotsky's perspective, I have provided you with an example study.

A researcher in Bolivia aimed to measure the creativity of children from different backgrounds, comparing two groups: rural children with no access to television and urban children with television access. The researcher asked them to draw pictures at home and bring them to class for comparison. The researcher collected these drawings and compared them. The results of the study showed that rural children had significantly less diversity in their drawings, predominantly depicting pets and limited items in their surroundings. However, children with television access drew images that were not present in their immediate environment, displaying a much greater variety in their drawings. Interpreting these research findings based on Vygotsky's perspective, it can be argued that this reality demonstrates the positive influence of television on the creativity of children who have access to it.

Based on this premise, animations, books, and films can serve as primary sources for fostering creativity. They provide the raw material for children's imagination, enabling them to ultimately create new visualizations. However, this does not hold true for children of all ages. Research indicates that films and animation, especially in combination with relevant toys, stimulate the imagination of young children who are not yet capable of doing so personally. However, it can hinder the imagination of older children who have a greater age and more advanced cognitive skills.

Therefore, it is predicted that films and animation can serve as creative stimuli for young children when they are not capable of doing so themselves. However, as children grow older and go to school, it is important to assist them in developing their visualization and imaginative abilities without relying on television.

Typically, children under the age of 6 possess better creativity compared to adults. This can be attributed to the fact that their minds have not yet become accustomed to the physical rules and structures that exist in the world. Consequently, their minds are more liberated from constraints and can be more creative. However, over time, their minds adapt to these structures and rules, making it more challenging to be creative for a mind that does not engage in creative exercises.

For this reason, around the age of 5 or 6, it is crucial to actively work on fostering children's creativity and limit their exposure to animations and films. However, it is also essential for you as a parent or caregiver to be a creative individual yourself. Practice creativity with the child and encourage innovative ways of thinking!

In summary, television stimulates children's creativity until the age of 7 or 8, but beyond that age, it can make them passive, and without engaging in creative activities, their creativity may decline. In fact, since movies and TV present ready-made images to children, if we fail to prepare their minds for active engagement with these images, it can potentially undermine their creativity and be detrimental. In this regard, parents and caregivers can utilize television to enhance their children's cognitive abilities through mediation between their child and TV. They should exhibit three types of behaviors in their mediation efforts:

- Engaging in conversations with the child about the content of television programs.
- Establishing rules or limitations regarding television viewing or restrictive mediation.
- Watching television together with the child or engaging in shared viewing experiences.

In the process of these mediations, media literacy education is happening, and, in fact, the purpose of these mediations is to improve children' media literacy.

Ultimately, it should be noted that different types of media sell dreams to children. Children cannot always be consumers of dreams; instead, we should help them become self-sufficient in dream weaving over time. It is crucial to reiterate that cartoons and films can serve as one of the sources of raw materials for children's creativity, but that's it! This means that watching cartoons and films cannot make them creative unconditionally; children themselves must also practice being creative. It is essential to mention that creativity is not limited to producing a specific art form; it can involve creating an imagination, crafting a short story, offering a new perspective on a subject, devising a new way to return home, finding a solution to a problem, painting a new artwork, developing a new way of kindness, creating a short animation, capturing a new angle in a photograph, etc.

Roleplay as a Director

A great activity to stimulate a child's mind is to give them the opportunity to be a writer and director. Ask them to tell a story, and you can write it down on paper. Then assign different roles to family members and ask them to perform their roles as you read the story. Additionally, inquire about the appearance of the characters, their inner traits, and their relationships, helping them refine and enrich their story. Questions about this story can invigorate child's mind:

- What do the characters like to wear?
- Do they have any special powers?
- What is their relationship with each other? Are they a family?
- What events happen between them?
- Do they like each other?
- Is there a problem that challenges them together?

By engaging in such activities and asking these questions, you can enhance the child's creativity and imagination.

Utilizing Voice Recording

Use the voice-recording feature on your mobile phone to engage with your child. Sing songs, have conversations, create interesting sentences, generate imaginative words, and record them. Pause the recording briefly and allow your child to enjoy the sounds they have created.

Or create a sound mystery. Produce different sounds by using tools or whatever is at hand and record them. Then play the recorded sound and ask each other to guess how the sound was produced or what the sound is.

For example, the sound of frying potatoes, when recorded, sounds like a downpour. Through this activity, you can enhance your child's creativity and engage in conversations about sound effects in films and how they are produced.

By utilizing mobile phone recording application, you can actively participate in creative activities with your child and initiate discussions about sound effects and their production methods.

Fostering Creativity through Illustrated Storytelling

Part of your responsibility as a parent or caregiver is to assist the child in telling their own story and expressing their perspectives through narratives. One effective method in this regard is using illustrated stories or comic strips (Figure 1). In this visual storytelling approach, the child can write their own story inspired by the images, within the panels. They can also draw their story in a series of interconnected panels and add text for the storyline and character dialogues in each panel. This exercise is beneficial for all ages and can serve as an exceptional recreational activity for fostering creativity and self-expression.

Figure 1 Comic script.

Writing a Story as a Creative Activity

According to Vygotsky (2004), creating the first drawing is an initial form of children's creative activity. Children's interest in drawing arises from their inner needs. Drawing provides them with an opportunity to express their concerns and thoughts. However, as children grow older and become adolescents (typically between the ages of 10 and 14), their interest in drawing diminishes, and this activity continues only among those who have a particular talent in this field or have specific stimuli around them to sustain their engagement in this activity.

Have you noticed that our drawing skills often remain at the level of a 10-year-old child?

After childhood, during adolescence, the interest in creative writing replaces drawing. However, this creative endeavor requires writing skill. If these abilities are not nurtured and strengthened, adolescents' interest in writing diminishes right from the start. Therefore, it is essential to assist them in developing writing skills from childhood.

There are various ways to cultivate this skill. As a starting point, we can describe the plots of short animated movies to each other. After a while, we can begin writing our own stories and read them to one another. Over time, we can extend this exercise to longer animated movies and strive to conclude the story differently or introduce changes to it.

Furthermore, we can encourage children to write about events happening in their lives. You, as a parent, should engage in this activity as well. Undoubtedly, children find the sound of their parents' actions more appealing and pay greater attention to those sounds.

Creating Animation as a Creative Activity

Children spend hours of their time watching animations. We should spark their curiosity about how animations are made. To begin with, introduce the concept of frames to them. Each frame is an image, and when they are placed one after another, due to the persistence of vision, they create the illusion of movement. A ten-minute animation is composed of thousands of frames, and sometimes it takes up to two years to create a high-quality animation within that timeframe.

You can make the concept of frames more engaging by using something like a flipbook. A flipbook has a structure similar to a book, with a different drawing on each page. When quickly flipping the pages, due to the persistence of vision, the drawings appear to be in motion, and each drawing serves as a frame.

Attention! Just Listen

While watching a movie, cover the screen of the movie player and only listen to the audio. Afterwards, discuss how each of you visualized the scenes. You can also ask your child to draw the events that occur when the image is not visible (DeGaetano, 2004).

You can also reverse this activity by muting the television while watching a show and discussing the actions happening in the film. In other words, interpret the actions and imagine what else the characters could say to each other, regardless of the real conversation.

Stimulate Their Mind

Children under the age of 6 often imitate what they see or hear on television. The reason is their strong desire for learning which could be superficial and limited to verbal or visual imitation of television programs. For example, they may repeat their catchphrases or imitate their way of walking or dancing. When encouraging them to create their own dialogues or different stories, don't hesitate to ask them questions that stimulate their creativity. For example, ask them:

- What did happen at the beginning of the film?
- Which character would you like to be? Why?
- If you were the author, how would you finish the story?

Watch Films with Your Child and Engage in Conversation

My doctoral thesis was focused on studying children's interpretations of critical concepts in animations such as Inside Out, Happyfeet, Zootopia, Wall E, Frozen, etc. In my research I played animations for children that contained critical concepts such as breaking gender stereotypes and disability stereotypes, respecting differences, defamiliarization, the role of technology in human life, etc. Often, these concepts contrasted with the children's prior knowledge, and I wanted to understand how children interpreted these critical concepts presented in animations and how closely or distantly their interpretations aligned with the story.

I can confidently say that if animations and films contrast with the child's prior knowledge, they will never be fully understood by the child. Instead, the child will interpret them in a way that aligns with their prior knowledge. This means that films and animations alone cannot influence or contribute to the growth (or even have a negative impact on) a child unless those meanings and beliefs have already been scaffolded in the child's mind. Therefore, when a child watches a film, they primarily use it to reinforce their existing beliefs rather than to manipulate their preconceived mental frameworks. This essentially means that the film impact (positive or negative) on the child's cognition during the viewing process is conditional.

One of the important findings I discovered during the research was the significance of conversation in the caregiver-child relationship and child development. The missing link in utilizing these animations for a child's growth is dialogue. You need to turn the discussion and dialogue with the child into a ritual after watching the film. If that is not feasible after each animation, at least implement this ritual on certain occasions after watching the film. The conversation can revolve around the film's storyline, judging the characters, uncovering the film's assumptions, understanding its message, etc. This conversation does not mean conducting a formal classroom session for the child. In fact, you should position yourself on an equal footing with the child and engage in a philosophical discussion. Your aim should not be to overpower the child's thoughts; instead, focus more on asking questions rather than providing interpretations. The outcome is not of great importance; the key is engaging in the act of conversation, which enhances the thinking skills and reasoning abilities of both of you. Through this process, watching films becomes a catalyst for cognitive development and thinking skills improvement in the child, as well as in yourself.

Sometimes, after watching a film, ask the child to describe the film's story. In doing so, the child gradually grasps the concept of the story, pays closer attention to the film, and becomes more consciously aware of the process of watching the film.

Additionally, you can ask the following types of questions after watching the film:

- What are your thoughts about the film/characters/events?
- Why do you think that way?
- Do you have any reasons? How are you sure?
- Is it always like this? How?
- Is there any other method/reason/suggestion?
- What do you think will happen next?
- Which character did you like the most and why?
- How would you have preferred the film's story to end?
- Have you had any similar experiences to the film's characters?
- What mistakes do the film's characters make, and what are the consequences of those mistakes?
- If you were in character X's position, what would you do?

Furthermore, you can discuss filmmaking techniques with the child, such as how camera angles can ignore or even distort aspects of reality. These types of questions are open-ended and thought-provoking, typically not rooted in a definite answer, and they encourage endless and reflective responses.

An important point during conversations with the child is to be patient in the face of their silence (when they are thinking). A good response is worth the wait. In questioning, we should value silence; therefore, provide the child with the opportunity for thoughtful silence. This thoughtful silence is the essence of the discussion and is more important than the response itself.

Learning Conceptual Tools

Engaging in conversation with a child allows you to teach them more concepts. Concepts refer to words and vocabulary that serve as tools to help the child think better and more deeply. Often, these concepts can be found in films and animations. For example, animations serve as a treasure trove of conceptual tools for children. A conceptual tool is something we need for analyzing and making sense of the information we receive in the world. For instance, the word "prejudice" is a concept and a tool for analyzing human behavior. If a child is unfamiliar with the concept of prejudice, they cannot properly analyze a situation where they might be judged before being known. However, when they are familiar with the concept of prejudice and have categorized similar instances under that label in their mind, they can analyze such situations without feeling guilty or being burdened by external judgments.

The more words or concepts a child has in their mind, the better they can comprehend and categorize the information they receive, experience less ambiguity, and become more familiar with their own world. Teaching concepts to a child is equivalent to helping them understand personal, social, cultural, economic, and other issues. Films are one of the primary sources for teaching concepts to children. However, children cannot learn concepts solely from films because they usually do not learn the name of the concept rather, they see instances of concepts in films.

In fact, it is your responsibility to explain to them the meaning of a particular action in the films. For example, in the animated movie "Frozen," the character Christoff initially is indifferent toward Anna and avoids recognizing her worth. Furthermore, his behavior indicates that he has made judgments about Anna without getting to know her. Children generally cannot analyze Christoff's behavior because they lack the vocabulary for concepts such as prejudice and are unaware of gender stereotypes. If they understand these two concepts, prejudice and stereotype, they can easily interpret and categorize the information. In this animation, there is an example of prejudice, but it does not explicitly tell the child what this act is called. When watching a film with a child, teach them the concepts. Start by asking them what the action of character X represents, and if they don't know, explain the concept to them.

Always ask your child to describe their interpretation of the message conveyed by the animated movies after watching them. Keep in mind that you should not convey this meaning to the child that there is a definite answer regarding the film's message, and they should not strive to find that answer in your mind. The child should understand that the conclusion they reach on their own also holds value and authenticity because it belongs to them. This is how you can teach a child to think for themselves and seek answers within their own mind.

When it comes to questioning a child about the content of television programs, it is always good to present your own conclusions and discuss them with the children after they share their thoughts. Acknowledge their thoughts and value them. If we provide the child with ready-made conclusions instead of asking them questions and encouraging their thinking, their understanding of the program's content will undoubtedly be limited.

A Lesson Arising from a Mistake

When I ask children about the message of a film or story, they often respond in the form of a question. For example, they might say, "Was it about not harming the environment?" Implicitly, this response suggests that first, every film or story has a clear or specific message, and secondly, I possess a definite answer to that message.

For this reason, I have realized that this questioning approach is incorrect and creates a mental barrier for children. If our intention is for a child to think independently and conclude that they can reach through their own thinking, we need to use different words to ask the question. For example, we can ask, "What was your interpretation of this film?" or "What message do you think this film conveyed?" When I explicitly ask in my question, "What was your interpretation," rather than asking "What is the message?" I emphasize the child's role and consider them as the owner of their own thoughts and ideas. However, when I ask, "What was the message of the film," I implicitly assume a specific message for the film and then I ask the child to discover it. This type of questioning acts as a barrier to the child's thinking process.

Changing the question alone is not sufficient in our interaction with children because the habit of not thinking and accepting ready-made answers has become ingrained in some children. Some of them never consider themselves capable of having their own ideas and opinions, so they respond with a questioning tone at the end (for example, they might say, "Was the message not to lie?"). This response essentially implies that there is a definite answer, which is with me (the questioner).

These types of responses are resulted by the expectation of specific answers from children and the repeated affirmation after the child discovers something that was in the teacher or parent's mind. Teaching children to think in this manner can be challenging, but by valuing their opinions, we can gradually help them understand that they can think for themselves and have their own ideas and perspectives. There are various ways to accomplish this. One approach could be to say, "In my opinion (or my interpretation), the message of this film or story was[...] so, what is your opinion?" In this way, we share our own answer that already exists in our mind, so they no longer have to search for an answer that is in our thoughts. We should encourage them to move away from the assumption of a "single and definite answer" and help them realize that they can have their own specific response.

In general, engaging in conversations with children about films has positive outcomes for the following reasons:

- Children's learning occurs through interaction with humans. Research shows that when children are watching an educational program and their parents accompany them and occasionally facilitating their understanding, their learning is greatly enhanced. In these interactions, children develop social and language skills, learning how to respond to questions and participate in conversations.
- Active viewing skill is fostered. Active viewing refers to actively processing the messages received, reflecting on them, and engaging in internal dialogue. When you watch a film with a child and engage with them in conversation about that film, they gradually learn that they can learn many things from films, dismiss certain messages, and actively participate in message reception. Therefore, while watching a film, it is beneficial to ask them questions, share your experiences, and engage in discussions about the accuracy or validity of the messages. However, it is important to perform these activities in a way that does not frustrate the child.
- Conversations with open-ended outcomes are valuable. It is not necessary for your conversations to always reach a conclusive result while watching a film. Conversations that remain open-ended engage the child's mind and stimulate their thinking. It is better not to play the role of an all-knowing authority figure, but rather frequently encourage the child to find their own answers and share them with you.
- Child' critical thinking is strengthened. Developing critical thinking is a skill that requires practice and effort on the child's side. It is not something that naturally emerges from their experiences. Instead, it requires challenging their mind, engaging in thoughtful reflection, maintaining thoughtful silence, expressing their thoughts, and ultimately presenting their own thoughts derived from their mental processing. It is important to note that when we impose opinions on a child, we are not fostering critical thinking. The most effective approach to enhance this skill is through the practice of engaging in good conversations.

A Technique for Nurturing Thinking Skills: Employ Logical Language

Parenting skills are interconnected, much like a chain. If parents are unable to cultivate critical thinking in children, they will inevitably struggle to raise them as rational individuals in the face of technology. A rational individual is someone who purposefully utilizes communication technologies and interacts with them consciously.

The most effective approach to nurturing a child with logical thinking abilities, who can think critically, revolves around the use of language. Try to consistently employ logical connectors (therefore, thus, after, in conclusion, etc.) and argumentative phrases (because, since, consequently, etc.) in your communication with your child. When using this type of language, you naturally find yourself in a structure that compels you to engage with your child in a logical manner.

Furthermore, encourage the child to immerse themselves in this linguistic structure. When they ask you a question, respond to them in a logical manner but using their own language. If you disagree with something, explain your reasons to them (while incorporating logical connectors and argumentative words in your sentences). Apply this practice reciprocally and ask the child to explain their own reasons as well.

The character of a child who is treated in this manner develops in such a way that when you ask them why they want a tablet or why they want to join social networks, they provide you with logical justifications. Furthermore, this logic is also present in their internal dialogue with themselves.

Alongside this approach, you can utilize following suggestions to foster logical reasoning skills in children under the age of 5 or 6:

- Examining and labelling object features.
- Comparing objects, observing their differences and similarities.
- Utilizing and describing an object from various perspectives.
- Assisting in understanding logical and causal relationships and logical propositions such as "if…then."
- Sorting objects based on certain dimensions or relationships between them (e.g., tallest, or shortest).

Overcome a Major Obstacle to Improve Children's Critical Thinking

One of the barriers to critical thinking is the imposition of concepts created by the media in the minds of their audience, concepts that can mentally confine children. To understand my point, consider the following example: What characteristics do heroes typically have in animations and stories?

If you pay attention, you'll notice that they usually are often muscular, powerful, intelligent beings with supernatural abilities. They can fly, are usually male, and so on. The portrayal of heroes in books, movies, animations, and games creates a concept in the child's mind that restricts heroes to beings who possess these particular characteristics. In this case, we can say that this concept has become a conceptual dictatorship dictating the perception of children and only acknowledging individuals who possess these qualities as heroes. Consequently, this constructed concept of heroes prevents individuals with different traits from being recognized.

One of our main responsibilities is to recognize these dictatorship concepts. We must be able to identify all these concepts and dismantle them by providing examples, counterexamples, and logical refutations. The concept of a hero is just one of the numerous concepts that are constructed by the media. We need to improve this skill in children so that they can discover these concepts themselves. For example, related to the concept of hero, we can engage in a question-based conversation with the child and evoke numerous examples in their mind of individuals who cannot fly, are not muscular, are not male, or are not powerful, yet they are heroes. However, before doing so, we must first strengthen our own ability to recognize these dictatorship concepts.

A Secret about Film and Animation

When we perform a specific movement, mirror neurons in our brain become active. These same neurons are activated again when we simply observe that movement being performed by another person. For instance, if we see someone getting up from a chair, our brain simulates the act of getting up from a chair, but we do not physically get up ourselves. In essence, every movement we witness is mentally enacted in our brain (Torre, 2014).

Understanding this concept contributes to learning all the movements associated with the body and the ability to perform them, such as learning various dance styles, martial arts, sports activities, etc. This means that a part of our program for learning activities related to body movement should involve continuous watching of videos or live performances of those activities.

Utilizing Media to Enhance Interpersonal Intelligence

Interpersonal intelligence refers to the ability to understand others. One of the factors that limits children's intelligence is their egocentrism, the belief that the world revolves around them and their thoughts. Getting rid of being egocentrism is not something that naturally occurs with getting older; rather, they need to learn the skills to not assume themselves at the center of the world. There are many individuals who continue to believe in their adulthood that they are the center of the world, and the world revolves around their beliefs and perspectives. These individuals have very limited ability to understand others because they cannot see the world from others' perspective.

Humans need to start learning in childhood about the fact that people are different beings with their own personalities, spirit, motivations, and intentions. Interpersonal intelligence emerges from knowing this fundamental fact, and we observe its manifestations in social skills, empathy, and the ability to learn from others.

Some exercises to enhance this intelligence include:

- Allowing the children to immerse themselves in different characters from movies and express their emotions.
- Encouraging the child to express their opinions from the perspectives of various characters in movies, stories, and animations.
- Actively listening to others when they narrate stories, poems, provide information, or engage in discussions.
- When watching a movie or reading a story with the child, empathize with different characters, especially those who are victims.

Enhancing Metacognitive Skills in Children

An essential skill for critical thinking is metacognition. What I am sharing with you is highly significant for nurturing a child with the ability to reflect on their behavior and emotions through critical thinking. This entails a child who not only engages with media and communication technologies in a logical and controlled manner but also applies this approach to all aspects of life. A skill that needs to be strengthened in children in this regard is metacognition.

Metacognition refers to thinking about thinking. It means taking a step back and examining ourselves, reflecting on our behaviors, critically analyzing our emotions, and overall contemplating our thoughts, actions, and feelings. This extraordinary ability is unique to humans and, when enhanced, becomes a skill that fosters our development.

This skill helps us understand the impact of the online space on our behavior and beliefs. It helps us delve into why we may not be successful in a particular domain, or when we are deceiving ourselves, or what issues exist within ourselves that decrease our ability. Moreover, metacognitive skills assist us in finding solutions to the problems we identify within ourselves, which is related to problem-solving abilities.

Now, how can we cultivate children who can take a step back, reflect on their behavior, manage it, and improve this skill? I recommend strategies to enhance metacognitive skills in the realm of media usage and online space. I must emphasize that this skill can aid us in managing our behavior and emotions across all dimensions of life.

- Ask the children to think about why they use media and how it has helped them in achieving their goals.
- Inquire why they often turn to their mobile devices and tablets. Is it due to stress, addiction, aimlessness, or something else?
- Explore whether they can avoid using all forms of media for a while. If they can, ask them why many people struggle to abstain themselves from

using different forms of media. If their answer is no, inquire why they believe they cannot do it.
- Discuss the abilities, skills, and limitations they have discovered within themselves. Are these limitations truly inherent or might they have been imposed upon them?
- Explain the concept of metacognition to the child as a tool for thinking. Describe how this skill functions in human development. They will surely ponder upon it.

By doing the mentioned suggestions, you help children to reflect on themselves and their behaviors, which means you are nurturing this skill in the child!

Remember, parenting skills are interconnected like a chain, and if children are weak in certain skills, we cannot expect them to use media and communication technologies effectively. Metacognition is one of these links in the chain that is crucial for human growth at every stage of life. Let's cultivate this skill within ourselves as we accompany the child.

Talk about the Story Structure with Child

When reading a story or watching a movie with your child, engage in a conversation about the structure of the story. Assist your child in understanding that every story has structure. Generally, the structure of a story consists of the following elements:

- Plot (plot refers to the sequence of events that unfold)
- Actions and reactions of the characters and stimuli
- Story characters, protagonist, and antagonist
- Challenges
- Climax and resolution of the challenge.

Explore various characters in the story with your child and determine which character is the hero and which one is the antagonist. Identify the challenges faced by the hero and discuss their decision-making process for resolving those challenges. You can also ask your child questions such as:

- Did a particular event occur at the beginning or end of the story?
- What happened next? Why did the story's hero take that action?
- What was the antagonist's reaction?
- What were the story's challenges?

The Use of the Internet for Children's Growth

The Internet is one of those technologies that entered our lives before parents and children were fully prepared to face it. This technology, alongside all its potential risks, provides an incredible platform for sharing human knowledge and experiences. By educating children on how to use this technology, we can make them creative, curious, and empowered. However, parents should initially be mindful that their children should not have more mastery over the internet than themselves. But this does not mean you should hinder your children's learning in this area, so they always know less than you. Instead, despite the challenges that may arise due to age and mental distractions for your own learning, you should constantly seek to enhance your knowledge of the internet. Because only if you understand what the internet is and how to make the most of it, you will be able to play as a good mediator for your child to navigate the online world.

Children under the age of 6 should always use the internet with one of their parents or caregivers. When engaging in internet activities with the child, describe every action you take, and explain what is happening in a calm and organized manner. Provide explanations about how search engines work and guide them to websites and software that are beneficial for them. It is crucial to maintain constant supervision over their internet usage.

When your child starts school, the internet can serve as a valuable resource for their assignments. However, it is important to teach them that not all content found on the internet is reliable. You can ask your child to research a specific topic online and share their findings with you, and then together, you can verify the information using various sources, including the internet itself (I have written about how to evaluate information in Chapter 6).

It is essential to establish rules for internet usage at home, including specific hours and duration of internet use, as well as clearly outlining prohibited activities. It is crucial for children to understand the importance of protecting online privacy. Make them aware that using their real identity on websites and providing their email can pose risks. You can ask them about the potential dangers and how others may abuse such information. Your child should understand that anyone can operate with a fake identity on the internet while gaining the trust of others for malicious purposes. Over time, you should educate your child, preferably through research-based methods, about all the opportunities and risks that the internet presents.

Consider Book as a Media

It has happened many times that when I asked someone for a source during a discussion, they responded by saying it's written in a book or books. Since publishing a book is not as easy as posting something on the internet, most people tend to believe that books are more trustworthy. However, it is important to note that the content of books also requires verification because they might contain incorrect information. The process of publishing a book does not guarantee that its information has been fact-checked before publication. Therefore, to clarify this reality for children, it is necessary to have a suitable opportunity to discuss with them the process of publishing a book. This will help them understand that the content of books is not necessarily accurate and precise. In fact, just as we teach children to have a critical eye when it comes to movies, news, animations, and all forms of media, we should remind them that the content of books can also be flawed. Therefore, it is important to encourage them to critically evaluate and verify the information presented in books.

However, if you pay attention, you'll notice that there is a lot of advertising worldwide promoting book reading, and the reading rate is considered an indicator of development in societies. In these advertisements, reading books is equated with intellectual thinking, implying that reading books will make us thoughtful and knowledgeable. However, does reading books alone make us thoughtful and knowledgeable?

To answer this question, we need to differentiate between two levels of thinking: high-level thinking and low-level thinking:

- Low-level thinking includes awareness of information, comprehension of information, and application of information.
- Higher-level thinking includes analysis of information, synthesis (creating something new from previous information), and evaluation (thinking about the accuracy and correctness of information) (Bloom, 1956 quoted by Adams, 2015).

Can reading books alone facilitate higher-level thinking?

Both children and adults, until they are able to create new ideas from their readings, develop a new perspective, or critically evaluate the accuracy and correctness of the information they read in books, remain at the level of low-level thinking.

With this introduction, as long as we cannot generate a new perspective from what we read and evaluate the information we receive, we cannot achieve higher-level thinking. Any activity in which we are passive is considered low-level thinking. However, when we contemplate the information, we receive and reflect on its accuracy and correctness, we are truly engaged in thinking. Therefore, in this journey, not only books but also movies and animations can help us and children achieve higher-level thinking as long as we create our perspectives and are active in perceiving them. So, when we encounter advertisements emphasizing the importance of reading books, we should look at them critically.

References

Adams, N. E. (2015 Jul). Bloom's taxonomy of cognitive learning objectives. *Journal of the Medical Library Association*, 103(3), 152–153. https://doi.org/10.3163/1536-5050.103.3.010. PMID: 26213509; PMCID: PMC4511057.

DeGaetano, G. (2004). *Parenting well in a media age, keeping our kids human*. California. Personhood Press.

Torre, D. (2014). Cognitive animation theory: A process-based reading of animation and human cognition. *Animation*, 9(1), 47–64. https://doi.org/10.1177/1746847713519390

Verenikina, I., Herrington, J., Peterson, R., & Mantei, J. (2010). Computers and play in early childhood: Affordances and limitations. *Journal of Interactive Learning Research*, 21(1), 139–159. Waynesville, NC: Association for the Advancement of Computing in Education (AACE). Retrieved March 21, 2024, from https://www.learntechlib.org/primary/p/30381/

Vygotsky, L. (2004). Imagination and creativity in childhood. *Journal of Russian and East European Psychology*, 42(1, January–February), 7–97.

4 Confronting Stereotypes in Media as Obstacles to Critical Thinking

Media Stereotypes

During the time as humans living in caves, we faced numerous dangers. Both wild and predatory animals posed significant threats to our lives, as stinging insects, and crawling creatures. To navigate through such dangerous circumstances unharmed, we required a mental ability: the power of categorizing everything we saw, heard, smelled, and experienced. We needed to quickly identify dangerous predators by creating a mental image of any menacing qualities they possessed. For instance, any creature with spots on its body, long sharp teeth, and swift movements was deemed hazardous, while any creature that crawled, was large, and emitted a loud, harsh sound necessitated our avoidance.

We acquired this information through experience, meaning that after some members of our group were attacked by creatures such as bears and tigers, we realized that any other creature resembling those predatory animals was also dangerous. It was necessary to categorize these classifications regarding food, trees, weather, and essentially anything related to our lives. In general, with this ability, we no longer needed to experience everything to determine whether it was good or bad, dangerous or safe, tasty or unpleasant. This ability made our lives easier, allowing us to make quick decisions, such as determining whether an individual from another tribe we encountered was dangerous or not. These categorizations are the same patterns that have now become much more extensive. How we establish communication with a new person, how we eat our food, how we take care of ourselves, what situations are dangerous, what situations are safe, and essentially all the knowledge we possess are our schemas.

Schemas are a network of interconnected thoughts, concepts, or relationships stored in individuals' memories that enable them to absorb and comprehend new information. Humans construct these schemas through interaction with their environment. In other word, a schema is a mental framework that individuals employ to interpret what they see and hear. A schema organizes perceptions and behaviors, enabling individuals to understand their

DOI: 10.4324/9781003528685-5

surroundings. The information we gather from the environment is mostly stored in the form of organized structures in the mind, rather than discrete elements or fragments (Singer & Revenson, 1996).

The ability to create schemas has been inherent in humans and has aided in our survival. As our lives have developed in various dimensions, this ability has proven beneficial, as we classify all information in our minds, eliminating the need to repeatedly experience and understand everything in different situations. However, this very capacity, which is valuable and useful, can also turn against us. Under what circumstances does this practical and positive ability become dysfunctional and negative?

To answer this question, I need to explore the realm of stereotypes. Our stereotypes about various subjects, such as women, men, ethnicities, nationalities, LGBTQs. etc., are considered part of our schemas. Our minds construct them to facilitate the easier classification and processing of the information and data we receive. When we attribute characteristics to individuals based on their gender, ethnicity, occupation, nationality, or appearance, we are creating what is commonly known as stereotypes. It means that we assign certain characteristics to someone, and we make judgments about them before even interacting with them. Before getting to know the person, we rely on the same categorizations that we have previously established in our minds, avoiding putting much effort into understanding them and relying on our previous information to form our perception of them. The formation of these frameworks is almost an automatic process that takes shape within our minds. Unless we consciously engage with this mental activity, these stereotypes persist as a flawed reference for judging individuals.

Now, why does this capability lead us to make mistakes and result in inaccurate conclusions? The reason is that classifying human beings is challenging, because they are not as predictable as classifying objects, animals, plants, and similar entities that are typically preprogrammed and remain unchanged over time. For example, it is impossible for a lion cub to transform into a full-grown leopard. Likewise, the transformation of an apple sapling into an orange tree is not feasible. However, it is possible for a child born into a criminal family in a disadvantage area to transform into a successful individual who can play a highly beneficial role in society.

Humans possess numerous potential capabilities, and these very capabilities allow them to exhibit different performances under similar conditions. Humans grow in diverse and varied circumstances, making it challenging to easily classify them. In other words, it is not possible to categorize their behavioral and mental attributes without error. For instance, we cannot simply state that individuals with disabilities are helpless and pitiful, women are weak, men are aggressive, doctors are money-driven, etc. Each person has the opportunity to become anything they desire, and we cannot definitively claim that individuals, based on their gender, ethnicity, occupation, or similar classifications, will possess specific characteristics, whether positive or negative.

As I mentioned, we refer to these beliefs as stereotypes. Stereotypes encompass the beliefs, attitudes, and prejudgments that exist within a society or community. They are part of human cognitive schemas that attribute certain characteristics to all members of a specific group. These schemas serve as a reference in our social interactions and should not be overlooked. They are mental structures that simplify complex elements in the environment and facilitate understanding. In fact, they represent our natural inclination to judge new realities that we encounter based on realities we already know. However, it's essential to classify certain schemas as stereotypes to distinguish them from other schema functions that may be beneficial.

"Stereotype" is a term that has been used in printing. Initially, when printing began, a stereotype referred to a metal plate used as a template for printing. Words were engraved on this plate, and then paper was placed over it, creating words on the newspaper. This template enabled the printing of the requested copies in a consistent manner. The term "stereotype" is derived from this word. Another closely related term is "cliché" which is often used interchangeably with "stereotype." The word "cliché" originates from French and dates back to the 1820s. Interestingly, this term, like "stereotype," was a printing-related term and referred to pre-made metal blocks used to reproduce words or images uniformly. Thus, it can also be understood as meaning 'pre-prepared' or 'extensively used.'

Considering that these clichés were pre-made and allowed for the consistent production of images and texts in large quantities, a psychiatrist named Robert Lifton introduced the term "cliché" into the literature of psychology in his book. He used this term to describe and facilitate the understanding of cognitive schemas or mental clichés. Lifton (1989) states that a cliché serves as an obstacle to thinking and is often prevalent in societies with ideological environments that demand conformity of thought. In such environments, the most complex and difficult problems of human beings are compressed into easily retrievable fixed formulas and slogans. Clichés are typically concise, clear, and generalized; they offer simplistic answers to complex questions and prevent us from thinking critically.

So far, I have explained what schemas are, when we refer to them as mental clichés or stereotypes, and the origin and essence of these two concepts: cliché and stereotype. Now, I aim to elaborate on the role of media in the reproduction of these clichés and how we can foster critical thinking about these clichés in children.

Media can both generate and reproduce these clichés and stereotypes. In other words, the media may repetitively present a particular image or stereotype about ethnicities, nationalities, genders, or other groups, to the extent that it becomes a cliché and a standardized perception within a community. This is the moment that we assert that the media constructs reality, meaning that they convey something that does not exist in our external world but through constant repetition, the media gradually transforms it into a reality in our minds.

However, in most cases, the media reproduces the same stereotypes that exist in the external world. This behavior can largely be attributed to the structure of the media, meaning that the structure of media and content production, whether it's in the form of film or news, inadvertently or deliberately becomes a promoter of clichéd perceptions. But how does this happen?

Given that most television programs are relatively short, the authors need to quickly establish the identities of the characters. To accomplish this, they rely on clichés, creating a fixed or conventional image of a person or group that has already been associated with the intended description. For example, if they want to portray a truck driver, they design a cap hat for them and depict them with a large belly and strong triceps, providing the necessary information to link this image with viewers' pre-existing knowledge of a typical truck driver. The danger of clichés lies in their potential to influence the viewer's perception of the represented group. If clichés are excessively exposed, they can contribute to discrimination against the portrayed group, deprive them of certain privileges in society, or subject them to mistreatment.

There are stereotypical beliefs that women are not good at math, men cannot cook. Or, an attractive man is often stereotypically portrayed as tall, muscular, kind, and slightly aggressive. Such representations of men can make those who do not fit this pattern feel inadequate, reinforcing the overall stereotype. The same applies to women. In most cases, these stereotypes have roots in the real world, meaning that the stereotypical belief already exists, and the media perpetuates and reproduces it.

Stereotypical representations may present a positive image of various human groups, but if these images continue to increase and fail to represent differences, they become stereotypes and impose limitations on individuals. For example, in the past, Hollywood animations portrayed girls as weak, creating a stereotypical image of all girls. However, nowadays, girls are often portrayed as superheroes in films and animations. These stereotypes gradually shape our ideal definition of an ideal woman based on being strong, simultaneously beautiful, and muscular. The media should represent all types of groups, not just specific ones. Otherwise, stereotypical beliefs form, imposing significant burdens on certain groups of individuals who do not possess those traits.

Strategies to Challenge Stereotypes

One should be cautious of unrealistic images of men and women in movies, animations, computer games, and other media. According to research, computer games display more unrealistic body images than any other medium. Many games also endorse violence against both women and men. If your child engages in such games, discuss with them about different characters and the acts of violence portrayed. When children see their parents expressing their critical views about these images and ideas, they become more sensitive and will inevitably think critically about the negativity associated with these images and events in the game.

Furthermore, media imagery can also be utilized to break gender stereotypes. Research on female scientists indicates that the early years of childhood are crucial for creating the possibility in girls' minds that they can aspire to be scientists, astronauts, engineers, etc. Showing them the portrayal of female scientist characters in television programs can assist preschool girls in learning that being a scientist can be an important profession for women. However, teaching the same message to adolescent girls through the depiction of female scientists in similar series is not as effective to the same extent.

The more we familiarize girls under the age of 6 with successful female characters, the more successful we will be in breaking gender stereotypes in their minds. Additionally, we create patterns in their minds that help them envision themselves as successful individuals in any field they desire in adulthood. Children, especially those aged 3–6, are the most susceptible group to accepting stereotypical beliefs, and their mental effort to categorize people and their characteristics leads to the formation of stereotypes quickly. In general, the early years of childhood are the time for the formation of stereotypes, and if cognitive skills of recognition and resistance against them are not taught during this period, erasing them from their mind in the future will be so challenging.

It is important to mention that gender stereotypes do not only exist in media and computer games, but they can also be present in physical games that children engage in. These stereotypes about games can hinder the opportunities for the cognitive development of both boys and girls. Extensive research has shown that there are no significant differences between infant boys and girls, aged 18–24 months, in the types of games they play and their preferences for toys. At this age, they enjoy playing with dolls, cars, trucks, and other toys, and no differences in their preferences for television programs are observed. However, around the age of 3, differences gradually emerge, as girls and boys start participating in separate and different activities. They refrain from playing with toys that they perceive as being associated with the opposite gender (Valkenburg, 2011).

As they grow older, these differences become more pronounced and evident. Boys tend to prefer combat-oriented games and show more interest in solo play, competition, and destruction. These differences are also reflected in the films they watch. They are more inclined toward action movies, sports-related content, fantasy violence, and risky scenarios. They also show a preference for male characters with supernatural powers. However, girls are more engaged in games that have caregiving elements, such as playing house or games that focus on relationships in general. They are more interested in creating rather than destroying and show a greater preference for calmer games rather than action-oriented ones. Their preferences for films also differ. They are attracted to musicals, princesses, fairies, and similar themes.

However, it should be noted that while boys are generally drawn to male hero characters, girls are interested in heroes of both genders (Valkenburg, 2011).

Since experience is essential for the development of our brains and mental abilities, just like food that is essential for our physical growth, genderizing games, colors, activities, and so on, deprives individuals of both genders of a significant portion of experiences that could be crucial for their cognitive development and the growth of their abilities. In other words, the differences that emerge in the preferences of girls and boys lead to them having distinct experiences. We should be able to encourage them to engage in each other's activities, thereby fostering life skills in a healthy and equitable society.

Just as boys need to develop their empathy and acquire these skills to establish healthy relationships with others, girls should also learn to fight and take risks at times. Just as boys need to learn how to construct, girls should also learn how to destruct. Genderizing games, colors, entertainment, and films contribute to the perpetuation of an unequal and unhealthy society. The objective is not to make people similar to each other, but rather to bring the minds and hearts of individuals closer together. They should grow according to their capabilities while being able to engage in compassionate interactions with society.

Counting Characters

When watching television or playing computer games with your child, initiate this research with your child:

- How many women are there?
- How many men are there?
- Is there a disabled person in the film?
- Is there any correlation between the characters' ethnicity, race, or gender and the way they are portrayed? For example, do all women in that film have specific characteristics? What about men? Also, individuals with disabilities or different ethnicities?
- Can you recall another movie/animation or any other type of media that has portrayed genders like this?

Discuss the results you have obtained with your child and analyze them together. Through this type of conversation, you help your child approach media more consciously and provide opportunities to discuss stereotypes with them in the future.

A Practice with Children Aged 5–8

Children in the age range of 5–8 years often have a great interest in categorizing things, characters, and events in black or white, i.e., bad or good. Their strong inclination to watch films with characters that are either extremely feminine or extremely masculine is also derived from this characteristic. In this regard, they have a strong interest in watching films where people are either very good or very bad, which we refer to as stereotypical and clichéd representations.

They enjoy quickly labelling a specific group of people as either good or bad, exhibiting a completely black-and-white thinking pattern. This type of thinking and tendency for categorization is a sign of a non-critical mind. If not addressed, this habit of categorizing and black-and-white thinking can persist in an individual.

One practice to develop critical thinking skills in children is to ask them to provide reasons and evidence to support their beliefs. Encourage them to give numerous examples and find counterexamples—examples that may indicate that their beliefs are incorrect. These situations can vary for each family in different places and circumstances. Identify these situations and use them as opportunities for the child's development.

A Practice to Challenge Disabilities Stereotypes

According to the words of Rumi, "The cure is where the pain is made." While it is true that the media perpetuates many stereotypes, there are countless opportunities in the media to confront these mental stereotypes and overcome them. For example, watch the Paralympic Games with your child. Observing these games provides a great opportunity to shape a positive and informed perspective in children regarding disability. When children witness the proud and capable face of a blind skier, it becomes impossible for them to view blind individuals with pity or inject a sense of powerless into the blind community.

When I ask children about their attitudes toward disability, those who have seen at least one successful blind person say that blind individuals are not weak. Therefore, they do not feel pity toward them, indicating that exposure to successful disabled individuals to the extent that it shapes a humane and accurate perspective helps children. However, the crucial point here is that children under the age of 9 generally need to see all types of successful disabled individuals to shape a good perspective toward disabled community.

The reason for this necessity is that they are at an age where realities need to be demonstrated to them through non-verbal means, as simply stating that individuals with disabilities can be capable does not have a significant impact on shaping their attitudes in a positive direction. Therefore, obtain the broadcast schedule of Paralympic games from the internet, watch them with children, and shatter stereotypes. As the saying goes, being blind is a neutral reality, but disability is a cognitive framework that society imposes on those who are blind. Being unable to walk is also a neutral reality, but incapacity is a cognitive framework that an individual creates for themselves. Therefore, the Paralympic Games provide a great opportunity to prevent the formation of these kinds of cognitive frameworks in children.

Another approach to challenge clichés about disability is to, for instance, ask children about their perceptions of people with disabilities in the real world. Then, ask them to pay attention to the images of disabled individuals in the movies and animations they watch, specifically how these films represent them. Once they have identified these characteristics, if they are found to be clichéd or negative, you can provide them with counterexamples or encourage them to find counterexamples themselves. This exercise can be conducted in various situations. Keep in mind that children's understanding of stereotypical perceptions will evolve over time, so give them the opportunity to engage in critical thinking on this matter.

References

Lifton, R. J. (1989). *Thought reform and the psychology of totalism: A study of 'brain-washing' in China*. The University of North Carolina Press. Chapel Hill, NC.

Singer, D. G., & Revenson, T. A. (1996). *A Piaget primer: How a child thinks* (Rev. ed.). New York. Plume.

Valkenburg, P. (2011). *Children's responses to the screen*. London: Lowrence Erlboum Associates Piblisher.

5 Safeguarding Children; Addressing Children's Fear from Films Characters and Protection from News

Media, Fear, and Anxiety

During my childhood in the 1970s, there was a cartoon called "Huckleberry Finn" that used to air on TV. The cartoon revolved around a boy named "Huck." Huck's father was a wicked and malevolent character who subjected Huck to a great deal of abuse, ultimately driving him to escape from home. In those days, Huck's father served as a significant source of fear for me, leading to numerous nightmares. However, I never discussed my fear with anyone, not even my parents. In fact, I was unaware that I should talk to someone about it, and my parents, like many others, never realized how terrifying this cartoon could be for children of my age.

Childhood fears are among the worst emotions one can experience in life. Animated movies and other forms of programs can be significant sources of fear for children and even adults. But how can we help children overcome these fears?

It is important to note that fear stimuli vary according to children's age. Typically, according to research, Preschool children between the ages of 3 and 6 fear animals, darkness, supernatural beings such as ghosts, ugly and wicked characters, kidnappers, monsters, and witches, as well as anything that appears strange or moves suddenly (Konkabayeva et al., 2016; Muris et al., 2000). However, the fears of children aged 8–12 are fear of darkness (sometime) and mostly related to physical injury and the death of family members. Adolescents also fear physical injuries and their fears resemble those of adults to a greater extent.

To be more specific, children ages 4–6 are considered a distinct group because, according to Piaget's theory of cognitive development, they are in the preoperational stage. In this stage, their cognitive abilities are limited, and they experience anxiety related to immediate, concrete threats. Additionally, children in this stage engage in magical thinking, which leads to fears of imaginary creatures. From age 7 onwards, children transition into the concrete operational stage. During this stage, which lasts until about age 12, children develop the ability to understand physical cause-and-effect relationships and

DOI: 10.4324/9781003528685-6

anticipate potential negative outcomes, expanding the range of stimuli that can provoke fear (Muris et al., 2000).

Research indicates that the effects of media programs on children's attitudes and behaviors are largely influenced by their perception of the realism of those events (Huston et al., 1995). Therefore, the ability to distinguish between imagination and reality is an area that requires attention to alleviate these fears in children. In fact, one of the most significant factors contributing to preschool children's fear of television characters is their inability to distinguish between fantasy and reality (Martarelli et al., 2015), often stemming from a lack of discussion about this topic by the people around them. As young children do not have a clear understanding of the television mechanism, it impacts their perception of television programs realities, and one consequence is that television programs and the characters within them can become a significant source of fear for them. In fact, if we do not engage in conversations with them about the difference between imagination and reality and do not show them through "visual" methods what is real and what is unreal, it may take until around the age of 7/8 for them to develop sufficient awareness of the distinction based on their own experiences.

Visual Strategies to Decrease Fear

You may have watched programs alongside your child that you found frightening for them. Therefore, in order to reduce your child's fear, you might have said, "Don't be afraid! It's not real." However, such statements invalidate their fears and do not necessarily calm young children. Also, saying phrases like "You shouldn't be scared" can make the situation more difficult for the child and severely undermine their self-confidence. This occurs because they might perceive their fear as a sign of weakness, and this feeling can result in a sense of inadequacy. There are other ways of invalidating children's fears and not accepting them, including both explicit and implicit verbal messages, redirecting the child, the use of metaphors, controlling through fear, and accepting some emotions but rejecting others (Sorin, 2003).

Understanding strategies for alleviating children's fears at different ages is crucial. For preschool-age children, "visual strategies" are the optimal choice. Instead of explaining why a certain character is not real or why they shouldn't be afraid of it, practical methods should be employed to teach children the distinction between reality and fiction. Verbal explanations (cognitive approaches) are not particularly effective since these young children have limited comprehension abilities. However, the mentioned method facilitates the process of "visual desensitization." For example, it can be beneficial for children to witness the transformation process of scary television characters through makeup. Additionally, showing children how animations are created and emphasizing that there is no need to fear them because they are not real can be helpful (Kundanis, 2003).

The most effective solution is to prevent children from watching horror movies. However, since we have limited control over visual stimuli to prevent them from watching such content, however, we do not exactly know which characters are frightening to our child, practical methods have proven to be more effective in addressing their fears.

From the perspective of young children, everything appears as they see it on the surface. Therefore, in their view, attractive characters are appealing, while unattractive characters are perceived as bad. It is very challenging to make young children understand that someone with a frightening appearance can be kind, whereas someone with an attractive appearance may pose a danger. The only way to convince young children is to find counterexamples and demonstrate them to the child.

We might assume that a young child would be terrified by an apocalyptic movie or a film depicting a nuclear attack. However, if the visual representation of these fears does not create a sense of horror for the young child, such as the fear evoked by a monster within them, then it is possible that the child may be less frightened by such a program compared to an adult or an older child (Kundanis, 2003).

Do Not Be Afraid! It's Not Real

Cognitive strategies are effective for children of older age. In fact, cognitive strategies involve talking to the child about frightening stimuli and engaging in discussions about the fictional nature of television's scary characters. For example, explaining why a Zombies are not real can significantly reduce their fear, or discussing how facial makeup can make an actor appear frightening. Older children are more comfortable discussing their fears verbally and can be convinced through verbal communication as well.

It is important to note that your child does not necessarily have to be afraid of a specific character to start educating them about the imaginary and real aspects of television programs/animations and other types of media. These lessons, which are part of media literacy education, should be provided to children. As a parent, you should persuade your child using appropriate methods to make them understand how and why scary media characters are not real and cannot harm us.

Develop Children's Resilience to Handle News

Autumn of 2017 marked a period when numerous news about missing or abducted children were circulating on Iranian social media networks. One of the reasons was because of a tragedy that occurred when a thief stole a car, unknowingly with a child inside. Sadly, the police later discovered the child dead. Popular Instagram pages and Telegram channels were filled with posts and discussions about incidents and the lost children. Almost everyone who had access to these pages and channels was aware of these cases. One evening, while cycling with my friend during this period, we heard a woman screaming. All eyes turned toward a shop where a young lady stood, crying out, "My child is missing! Where is my child?" Distraught, she traversed the width of the street, halting cars, confronting pedestrians, and shouting, "They've taken my child." Beside this distressed mother, there was a calm 6 or 7-year-old girl carefully scanning the surroundings. However, whenever her eyes met her frantic mother, she would burst into tears and follow her across the street. A large crowd gathered, and the police arrived, but just at that moment, like a hero, a little boy emerged from the arms of a woman and joined his mother amid the crowd!

The story went as follows: The 2-year-old boy went to the fitting room and got stuck there while his mother was busy browsing through the store's merchandise. After an extensive search of the entire shop, he was found there.

The mother, who for few minutes lost sight of her son, immediately fears that he may be lost or potentially abducted by someone. This unconscious pattern constructed in her mind creates a rule that any child who goes missing has been taken by a kidnapper, and the likelihood of finding the child alive no longer exists. Consequently, she dismisses other possibilities and does not consider the simplest action, which is a thorough search of the store.

Take a closer look at this particular incident. People would not read anywhere on any Instagram page, in any newspaper page, or on any news website that the lost boy was found after five minutes in the fitting room. However, if he wasn't found, people would certainly come across news of it somewhere! This illustrates the mechanism of news formation, which influence our mindset regarding the world we live in.

This very mechanism of news production is what causes us to predominantly be exposed to negative news, not good news! Today, millions of people got in their cars, travelled distances, and arrived safely at their destinations. Today, millions of children played on the streets, yet none of them were abducted. Today, thousands of good things happened, but none of them made the news. However, it only took one unfortunate incident to occur, and it would certainly be turned into a news story; a story that could have a role in shaping our mindset about the society we live in. All these aspects are related to the process of news selection, something we all need to understand and be aware of in this saturated world of news—how certain news stories are chosen (by an official or unofficial media outlet) to be published.

Understanding the reality of news selection is the most critical aspect one must grasp in the field of journalism. In a world saturated with information, it is paramount to acknowledge that news does not reflect a fair representation of various topics and events. Instead, certain events consistently acquire greater news value and are disseminated. This mechanism is not exclusive to official media outlets alone; ordinary citizens, who have access to social networks, also engage in the dissemination of news based on their own news values. These news stories influence our mindset about the world. Therefore, it is imperative to be fully aware of how they are formed. Consequently, it is essential to educate children about the news values that act as gatekeepers, determining which news is allowed to pass through and be shared with them.

Children should:

Understand that news is selective and biased, meaning that each media outlet chooses which news to cover and which events to overlook. Therefore, news is not impartial and does not encompass the whole truth; rather, it is a selection of truths. As a result of this knowledge, children will come to comprehend how this selection process occurs in the representations of mass media, and they will begin to understand how social values and biases influence these choices. Remember following points when teaching children how news work:

- Have a critical perspective on the news production process.
- Recognize the limiting factors in news production and their impact on the final news.
- Understand the concept of news gatekeeping and the role it plays in news selection.
- Know that the media usually wants to keep the audiences, and this influences how news is selected and constructed.
- Be aware of the influence of limiting factors on news distortion.
- Understand the structured nature of news and how this characteristic could change the meaning. For example, to make children aware of how structured television and radio interviews are, we should discuss some limitations like time constraints that force producers to delete or add certain content to adhere to a structured format. (For instance, in a program that only lasts ten minutes, many adjustments are likely made to fit the structured time frame.) We should engage children in discussions about these constraints, their effects on meaning we get from them, and the possibility of editing audio files, outlining the necessary steps and how to make the process captivating. An effective approach would be to show them an example video and then explore where edits have been made.
- Ultimately, gain an understanding of the concept of representation. Representation means that media outlets are unable to present reality to us; rather, they re-present it. There is an external reality, and each media outlet presents parts of it as reality based on their own orientations and policies. This can result in distortion or even contradiction with reality.

Children should ultimately be aware of the potential effects of news on our beliefs, opinions, and perspectives of the world. So, they need to consider the mechanisms of news formation. Second, they should contemplate the consequences of the news they share in the online space and the influences of them on mental patterns of others who may potentially read our forwarded news.

Protecting Children from Negative News

As mentioned in the previous section, the criteria for news values often result in unfortunate incidents being selected and disseminated as news. Therefore, in a media-saturated world, we are constantly exposed to negative news. Avoiding distressing news is nearly impossible as they are omnipresent, on television, social media, family gatherings, etc. These sorrowful news stories disturb and sadden us all. However, digesting such news is even more challenging for children, especially those under the age of 6. Research indicates that children, for up to a year following widely covered distressing incidents, experience anxiety due to the impact of these incidents on society! But how can we help children maintain their mental well-being when they are exposed to such news? You can read some tips as follows:

- Do not expose them to distressing news, but also avoid keeping unfortunate incidents as a secret from them. Eventually, they will encounter distressing news at school or among their friends. Therefore, try to explain to them what has happened without displaying worry or fear.
- When they read or see disturbing news, try to be present with them to help them better understand the incident and prevent misunderstandings. Ask them how they feel to help them identify their emotions. You can assist them in labelling their emotions associated with hearing the news. Additionally, encourage the expansion of their vocabulary to help them express their emotions effectively.
- Remind them that good things also happen. Explain to them that the media often represent negative news and incidents, rather than positive events. There are many good things happening in the world, but the media doesn't talk about them because they think it's not appealing to their audience.
- Look at these events as an opportunity and have meaningful conversations with children. It's an opportunity to discuss the probability of losing loved ones and how people can find calmness in such times, as well as the fact that it's completely natural and good to cry when a person is sad.
- Distract their attention with fun games and activities. While completely shielding them from this news may be difficult, engaging in enjoyable activities after hearing bad news provides children with fewer opportunities to dwell on it and become more unsettled.
- Avoid showing your anxiety and transferring it to children.
- Do not read out news of terrorism aloud and limit the use of media outlets that broadcast news of terrorism in the presence of children.

- Provide reassurance to the child that safety is ensured for them and their family.
- Assist them in distinguishing reality from imagination. Certainly, they hear exaggerated and somewhat unreal accounts of bad news from their friends. Therefore, try to talk to children about this and understand what goes on in their minds to correct it.

Ultimately, children look up to their parents as heroes who can protect them from any danger. If they see you in a worried state while watching the news or discussing unfortunate incidents happening in the world, they become deeply concerned and feel insecure. Always be careful not to express your concerns about news you hear from various media outlets in front of children. Avoid talking about incidents in their presence and always present yourself calmly, assuring them that everything is in order and no threat endangers their lives.

Teach the Child to Verify Reliability of Information

In the past, raising children was like farming, but now, with the presence of new media, we need children to be hunters in order to observe information and make proper choices (Jenkins, 2009). So, encourage your child to question the accuracy of information in the online space. Help your child examine the validity and accuracy of topics, so instead of seeking the first answer for research, they can explore multiple sources and gain a nuanced understanding of different perspectives on the subject.

Always encourage the child to ask themselves the following questions when using the internet:

- Where is the primary source of this information?
- From what perspective do these pieces of information look at reality?
- What information is missing or omitted?
- Are there specific groups or ideologies that are not represented here?
- Is someone trying to sell me something?
- How does the information on this website (text, images, website design) influence my understanding of the topic I am reading about?

Sometimes assign your adolescent child the task of fact-checking various sources (websites, social media, television, etc.) regarding a recent news story they have heard. Comparing the available information about a topic from different sources can reveal the limitations and biases of a single source. It can also uncover the financial supporter of a website and, ultimately, help us determine the extent to which the presented information is accurate.

References

Huston, A. C., Wright, J., Alvarez, M. M., Truglio, R., Fitch, M., & Piemyat, S. (1995). Perceived television reality and children's emotional and cognitive responses to its social content. *Journal of Applied Developmental Psychology*, 16(2), 231–251. https://doi.org/10.1016/0193-3973(95)90034-9

Jenkins, H. (2009). *Confronting the challenges of participatory culture media education for the 21st century*. London: MIT Press Cambridge.

Konkabayeva, A. E., Dakhbay, B. D., Oleksyuk, Z., Tykezhanova, G. M., Alshynbekova, G. K., & Starikova, A. Y. (2016). Research of fears of preschool age children. *International Journal of Environmental and Science Education*, 11(15), 8517–8535.

Kundanis, R. M. (2003). *Children, teens, families, and mass media: The millennial generation*. Mahwah, NJ: L. Erlbaum.

Martarelli, C. S., Mast, F. W., Läge, D., & Roebers, C. M. (2015). The distinction between real and fictional worlds: Investigating individual differences in fantasy understanding. *Cognitive Development*, 36, 111–126, https://doi.org/10.1016/j.cogdev.2015.10.001

Muris, P., Merckelbach, H., Gadet, B., & Moulaert, V. (2000). Fears, worries, and scary dreams in 4- to 12-year-old children: Their content, developmental pattern, and origins. *Journal of Clinical Child Psychology*, 29(1), 43–52. https://doi.org/10.1207/S15374424jccp2901_5

Sorin, R. (2003). Validating young children's feelings and experiences of fear. *Contemporary Issues in Early Childhood*, 4(1), 80–89.

6 Teaching Online Ethics to Children

Online Ethics

The internet and communication technologies have permeated our lives without giving us the chance to define the ethics appropriate for the online space. We have encountered a world that sometimes contradicts our moral values, leaving us bewildered. Undoubtedly, you have already realized the power this space can wield and the extent of harm it can inflict on individuals in the absence of ethical principles. Numerous studies have been conducted in this field, and most of them indicate that since we may not see the other person in virtual space, we might have lower empathy toward them and easily cause harm. However, lacking empathy is not the only concern. Sharing an image without permission, copying content without attribution, cyberbullying, and many other actions are relevant to the online ethics concerns.

It is essential to teach children how to:

- Search effectively in the online space.
- Verify information, participate in communities.
- Understand how the internet works, what is news.
- How to evaluate their credibility.

Moreover, teaching them ethical principles in the online environment is equally important. Children should be educated on the importance of upholding values and norms and how breaking them can impact our lives, especially in the online realm. They need to comprehend the meaning of ethical values, their origins, and how they are learned and conveyed. Children should acquire skills for managing emotions during online interactions and practice preventing and resolving conflicts in their daily lives, both online and offline.

They should receive education about managing their privacy and reputation in the online space, as well as learning how to make appropriate choices regarding sharing others' content. Discussions should be held with children on how activities in the online realm, such as commenting and expressing opinions on social networks, posting and sharing information, can shape

DOI: 10.4324/9781003528685-7

their image and identity. They need to grasp the understanding that online activities, just like offline ones, can either enhance their reputation or lead to infamy.

In general, children should understand how their online activities reflect on their lives, and they should gain an understanding and insight into ethical behavior and managing their reputation in diverse online environments. They need to comprehend the importance of privacy management and consider ethical issues when sharing others' online content. Children should be aware of what plagiarism is or what behaviors are considered misconduct in the online space.

However, how can we teach these lessons to children? How can we instruct them to adhere to and remember these aspects? Establishing values and norms in the online space can be challenging. Since these values have not been completely established yet, and the consensus on ethics in the offline world does not necessarily apply online, institutionalizing them in children can be a difficult but achievable task. Values and norms need to be reaffirmed in the online environment. It is not simply a matter of transferring the same values and norms from the offline world to the online realm; it requires re-educating individuals within the online environment.

Before presenting solutions, it is crucial to understand the stages of moral development in individuals and provide age-appropriate ethical education in the online space.

According to Kohlberg and Hersh's (1977) perspective, moral development occurs in three stages, and it is not necessarily automatic that individuals progress to higher stages as they grow older. Advancing to each stage requires education. The stages are as follows:

- Preconventional stage: In this stage, individuals engage in desirable actions or refrain from actions considered morally unacceptable by societal norms and their motivation for obeying or avoiding is fear of punishment or desire for rewards.
- Conventional stage: In this stage, individuals become aware of social norms and rules. Their motivation to engage in ethical behavior or refrain from it is driven by the desire for conformity, pleasing others, following rules and social codes, and participating in social contracts.
- Postconventional stage: In this stage, individuals go beyond societal norms and establish their own moral values. These values can align with or contradict the values of the society they live in. The individual reaches a level of intellectual independence concerning ethical matters and regulates their behavior based on the values they personally believe in, transcending societal values.

Children typically go through the preconventional and conventional stages, and if properly nurtured, they enter the postconventional stage during adolescence. According to Kohlberg's perspective, many adults struggle to transcend these moral stages. It is important to note that the subsequent stages do not replace the previous ones, and even individuals in the postconventional stage may occasionally engage in actions driven by fear of punishment or desire for rewards.

Teaching Online Ethics to children

When discussing the teaching of ethics to children, it is important to consider at which stage of moral development they are. For example, children under the age of 9 generally respond better to clear consequences or explicit explanations of rules and regulations, whereas adolescents are more likely to be influenced by their knowledge and awareness of social values and norms (such as those present in their school or family) or their inclination toward a general moral principle. That is why, while it is necessary to establish clear rules and procedures at all ages, we should also pay attention to conveying implicit messages about cultural or ethical values to children.

It is crucial to educate children about the rules and regulations that exist in the online space. Additionally, it is important to establish household rules that also cover online behavior. Research shows that children who adhere to rules for various online activities at home engage in less risky online behaviors. However, simply knowing about the consequences of actions such as plagiarism, online sexual chat, or using the phone while driving does not guarantee that they will refrain from such behaviors. One potential reason for this could be their perception of the consequences as distant from their own reality. Furthermore, for adolescents at this age, it is more important to be involved with peer groups and engage in social contracts rather than fear of punishment or be motivated by rewards to perform a certain action. That is why establishing household rules regarding internet usage is essential, not because of the penalties for breaking them, but because these rules contribute to the transmission of family values and expectations regarding behavior.

In general, the areas that require attention when fostering ethical behavior in children in the online space include:

- Respect for others and empathy
- Responsible sharing of personal information
- Cyberbullying
- Copyright
- Plagiarism

In the following sections, I have written about each of these topics and provided relevant strategies for effectively managing them.

How Can Empathy Be Developed in Children?

One of the effective skills in promoting ethical values is the ability of children to empathize with others. Strengthening this skill depends on the age of the child. Kids start showing signs of empathy around 18 months old when they begin to grasp that other people can have feelings different from their own (Roth-Hanania, 2002). At this stage, the best approach to cultivate empathy in children is to seize opportunities for role modelling and engage in conversations with them about empathy.

When a child is engaged in an activity or witnesses a scene where someone becomes sad, happy, or afraid, provide a thorough explanation to the child about how and why that action has caused the person to feel sad.

When children reach the age of around 4, it becomes possible to engage in discussions with them about imaginative situations:

- How would X feel if someone took their toy away?
- What emotions might their friend experience if someone took their toy away?

These discussions can help children understand that other individuals, just like them, have emotions.

As children mature and become more sophisticated in their EU, they begin to make correct emotion inferences in non-stereotypical situations around 4 years of age. Here, children begin to understand that others may experience a different emotion from their own in a given situation. For example, children understand that other people may feel scared when encountering a large dog, even though they themselves may feel happy in the same situation (Tan et al., 2021). We can encourage children, around 4 or 5 years and above, to actively put themselves in someone else's shoes. This can be done in real-life situations as well. We can engage them in creative role-play and create scenarios where children imagine themselves in someone else's position.

In relation to the online space, the following tips, which can be discussed with children, are useful for enhancing their empathy:

- The individuals we interact with online are real people, even if we don't know them offline. Before speaking or typing anything, always consider that you are communicating with a human.
- Avoid responding immediately. When something upsets you, give yourself some time to let the initial feelings of fear or anger subside.
- Whenever possible, try to establish face-to-face communication with people in real-life settings. Remember that individuals in online space may not fully understand your emotions, which can easily escalate conflicts and create an intense atmosphere.

- Discuss your feelings about topics that occupy your mind in the online space with a family member or a friend.
- If you have a personal issue with someone online, refrain from publicly attacking them. Doing so will only exacerbate the situation and make it more difficult to resolve.
- Be aware of your emotions. It is challenging to make wise decisions when you are angry, fearful, or embarrassed. If your heart is racing and you are experiencing intense emotions, it's time to go offline for a specific time.

Sharing Personal Information of Others

One of the most critical ethical decisions individuals must make in the era of social networking is how to respect people's privacy and keep personal Information of others. Due to the interconnected nature of the services and platforms people use, whenever a friend shares something, people are put in a situation. They should make a decision whether to disseminate it or not.

The most important task for you is to approach every activity your child engages in online as an ethical matter. Encourage them to consider the rightness or wrongness of everything they do online. This fosters critical thinking and reflection on their online actions. For instance, when it comes to sharing others' information, they think about whether it is ethical to do so in specific circumstances.

Teach children to think before publishing any kind of information and consider its potential impact on others. It is best to have a conversation at home about a clear and transparent set of rules regarding the disclosure of others' information.

You can enhance your child's empathy skills through discussing the sharing of others' personal information. For example, you can advise your child to always consider how they would feel if someone else were to share the same information about them.

What should be kept in mind regarding the sharing of personal information is that the adolescence stage is the time when romantic relationships begin, and friendships deepen. In both situations, children or adolescents may make incorrect decisions about sharing others' personal information. For this reason, it is crucial to provide children and adolescents with education on healthy relationships and the ability to recognize unhealthy relationships in the online space.

Although explicit and clear rules can have an impact, children and adolescents are most influenced by the social codes of their peer groups more than anything else. Sharing others' personal information may occur when children or adolescents are excited and follow the actions of their peer group. We need to educate children on being aware of their emotions and how to manage specific emotional situations. Here, I refer not only to negative emotions but also include positive emotions such as joy, which can increase the likelihood of making wrong decisions. Adolescents can be taught to be aware of their emotions and feelings during emotional situations, benefit from calming techniques, and practice refraining from making decisions that affect others until they have calmed down; decisions such as sharing others' personal information.

Cyberbullying

One aspect related to online ethics is cyberbullying. Cyberbullying has become a widespread phenomenon in adolescence due to the rapid expansion of information and communications technology (ICT) (Smith et al., 2008), which can have negative effects on children, such as causing subsequent anxiety problems, self-harm, and suicide. There is still insufficient research in the area of cyberbullying. However, experiencing cyberbullying is a significant issue in children's lives, leading to various problems for them. The more these technologies advance, the more complex and widespread the phenomenon of cyberbullying becomes. It has been found that cyberbullying tends to peak at around 14 and 15 years of age before decreasing through the latter years of adolescence. They discovered that with social media and gaming platforms technically requiring users to be at least 13 years of age, it is notable that one in four (25.1%) of those very young teenagers have been cyberbullied recently (Hinduja, 2021). Victims may stop from attending school due to psychological pressure or resort to self-harm or even suicide.

In person and online violence exhibit fundamental differences. In the online space, unlike the offline environment:

- The perpetrator often remains anonymous.
- There is a potentially unlimited audience that would be aware of the violence.
- The immediate visibility of the victim's reaction at the time of the crime is absent for the perpetrator.
- There is an imbalance of power between the offender and the victim.

These traits increase the chances of cyberbullying because being anonymous online makes people less hesitant to engage in it.

In the physical world, a victim can stay anonymous, but in the online space, it is the perpetrator who is more likely to remain anonymous. These characteristics of cyberbullying and its high potential for destruction underscore the need for more thinking about this phenomenon.

Based on social cognitive theory by Albert Bandura (1989), self-blame bias exists for victims of any form of violence. For example, victims might say to themselves: "This happened because I am flawed, and this flaw is permanent, and I cannot change it." This self-blame bias can lead to negative psychological reactions. Bandura describes the process of moral disengagement in this theory, whereby individuals allow themselves to violate ethical standards. In social cognitive theory, the moral behavior of everyone involves self-regulatory mechanisms, judgment, response, and moral justification. This theory illustrates the cognitive processes that a criminal employ to justify their behavior. According to Bandura's theory, the technological world can diminish ethical commitments. The inability to observe the victim's reactions makes it easier for the perpetrator to commit the crime, allowing them to easily justify their actions as mere entertainment not as an action that harm the victim.

Cyberbullying can manifest in various forms, such as trolling, altercation, abusive messages, spreading rumours, or sharing personal content of others. In the following sections I explain them. I have gotten different pattern of cyberbullying from Mediasmarts (n.d) however, concurrently, I have expanded upon the concepts.

Trolling

This form represents the most common form of bullying and refers to individuals who are intrusive or abusive in the online world (the primary meaning of trolling is to provoke people in a way that makes them angry). This form of bullying can be either completely anonymous or partially anonymous. The harasser may or may not recognize their victim. This bullying situation can continue and even escalate into persistent assault and harassment until the harasser receives the desired reaction.

Altercation

In contrast to the previous form, in this model of online harm, individuals usually know each other both in the online world and in the real world. It is often difficult to determine the perpetrator and the victim in these circumstances. Here, two people initiate an online fight, and their friends back them up by intruding into the opposing side in online space. Adolescents, in most cases, do not consider these incidents as online harassment and bullying. This is a type of public quarrel that is carried out by friends and peers, and these adolescents' friends support them either online or through another person involved in the situation.

Harassment

When bullying takes on a personal aspect and persists over time, we can label it as "harassment." This pattern likely bears the closest resemblance to our traditional understanding of harassment and bullying, where an individual (or a group) is actively targeting and hurting another person.

One of the main differences between "altercation" and "harassment" lies in the fact that individuals involved in "altercation" have relatively equal "social power." When more individuals support one side of the conflict in "altercation" or when something weakens the social standing of one of the factions, the situation quickly transforms into "harassment."

Violence in Relationships

Lastly, violence within relationships is another form of harassment and bullying that can occur partially or entirely online. Adolescents engaged in romantic relationships might experience these behaviors from their partners. These behaviors include stalking, threats, impersonation, and ridicule on social networks, sending abusive messages, pressuring them for sexual relationships or sending sexy photos, and publicly humiliating them through social media.

While these actions usually occur between the harasser and the victim, in some cases, the harasser may involve a larger audience to exacerbate the situation (such as spreading rumors about the victim or sharing their private information). In the worst-case scenario, these actions may happen after a sexual assault rather than a relationship based on consent.

As follows, I have provided some methods of educating children to tackle various forms of online bullying and to prevent them from becoming online bullies themselves:

Encouraging children to be proactive and ethical upstander, meaning that if they witness unethical behavior, they should not remain passive and instead advocate for the victim. We can also teach them how to avoid being involved in bullying. The approach to delivering this education may vary depending on the child's age.

Teaching younger children to enhance their empathy and emotional well-being is the best way to cultivate ethical behavior in them. We should clearly and explicitly communicate our expectations regarding their behavior and help them develop ethical thinking based on organized social rules, codes, values, and norms rather than fear of punishment.

As they reach adolescence, gradually educating them about healthy relationships and discussing the characteristics of unhealthy relationships becomes important so that they can recognize healthy and unhealthy relationships. Children at this age are most sensitive to social norms; therefore, raising their awareness of different forms of bullying and coercion can be the most effective approach so they will not take them as norms.

During times when the situation of altercation is gradually transitioning into "harassment" efforts to mediate and calm the situation can be highly effective. Recording and reporting bullying activities is also useful, especially in situations where there is a clear process for reporting abusive behavior.

You can suggest to your child's school to establish a mechanism for reporting online bullying so that it can be addressed, and support can be provided to the victims. For example, they can create a section on the school website dedicated to reporting online bullying or introduce an email or phone number for this purpose.

If individuals who are being bullied and coerced do not receive support from others, they gradually come to believe that they deserve such treatment and harassment. Therefore, it is essential to prepare children to tackle these forms of online bullying.

Copyright

Respecting copyright means showing respect for the creator of an idea, book, photograph, film, painting, architectural design, or anything else that brings them credibility (financial or spiritual). We should refrain from publishing or copying it without their permission because such dissemination may result in financial or non-financial harm to the creator.

To teach children to respect copyright, we should first present it to them as an ethical issue. This means making it clear to children that this action can have victims and negative consequences, encouraging them to think about the negative effects and repercussions before engaging in any inappropriate behavior.

Children hold the belief that taking something from media companies is distinct from taking something from an individual, as they do not consider it to be the same act of stealing; therefore, we must explain to them that copyright law is an important way that allows artists and other individuals to earn income from their creations and enables them to continue their work. Teach children that when an artist creates a piece of work, they also become the owner and have the right to make decisions about it.

We should help children understand that websites that profit from illegal activities not only harm the creators of the works but often endanger the privacy and security of those who use such content. For example, hackers place links on websites that, once clicked, may steal your personal information. In fact, these websites are aware of users' greed for accessing free content, so they set traps for them.

Plagiarism

Plagiarism refers to using someone else's idea, article, book, design, etc., without acknowledging the creator and pretending to be the owner of that idea, thought, or work. Children growing up in a culture where copying and plagiarizing others' work is considered a normal practice may find it difficult to perceive plagiarism as an ethical issue. Experiments provide evidence that, by age 5 years old, children understand that others have ideas and dislike the copying of these ideas (Olson & Shaw, 2010). So, we can teach them about the concept of plagiarism when they are young.

Useful strategies to raise awareness in children to plagiarism:

- The framing of plagiarism as an ethical issue and the identification of victims through empathy is crucial. We need to convince children that plagiarism has its victims, including themselves, as they are deprived of learning opportunities when they fail to generate their own ideas and instead resort to stealing others' ideas. However, the person whose work is copied is also a victim.

- Another solution is to ask children to remind themselves as content creators. For example, we can say to them, "Do you remember how you sold your handmade items (could be anything) at school? How would you feel if someone else copied them and sold them? Is that fair?"
- By presenting plagiarism as an ethical concern and encouraging empathy, as well as highlighting the role of adolescents as content producers, we can foster a deeper understanding and discourage such unethical behavior.

Additional Ttrategies for Teaching Online Ethics to Children

First and foremost, children need to understand what unethical behavior is. For example, they should be aware that copying content without proper citation is unethical. Or just as insulting people offline is considered unethical, the same applies to online spaces, even if our identity is anonymous. One way to internalize these values is to find suitable opportunities in everyday life to exemplify and train these ethics.

Provide conceptualizations for all forms of unethical behavior in the online space by giving them names. For instance, explain to children that copying content from the internet, books, or any other media without citing the source is considered plagiarism and is unethical. Or inform them about online harassment, bullying and other forms of cyberbullying. Essentially, we need to make the unethical instances clear to them. For instance, ask them, "Has anyone ever behaved badly or maliciously toward you online, making you feel bad? Have you ever said or done anything malicious or harmful to someone online?" Encourage them to provide examples of such behaviors, such as using specific names to refer to someone, threatening physical harm, spreading rumors, posting or sharing embarrassing photos or videos of a person, deriding someone's race or ethnicity, and other similar examples.

By providing clear definitions and encouraging children to identify and understand various forms of unethical behavior, we can effectively teach them about online ethics and promote responsible digital citizenship.

A crucial aspect of ethical education is to relate ethics to the child's own life. This involves asking them questions about their personal experiences and engaging in discussions about the consequences of their actions. Another important and effective approach is to utilize real-life stories for teaching ethics. When we are concerned about ethics, we are undoubtedly concerned about the harm that individuals may experience. Therefore, it is advisable to discuss with children the real-life harm caused by unethical behavior in the online world and share stories of individuals who have been affected by these harms.

Try to show children a picture of individuals who have been harmed or, if available, present an interview or video in which someone discusses the impact of online unethical behavior on their life. It is important to make that character as tangible and relatable as possible for the child. By narrating real-life stories to them, the tangible effects of online unethical behavior will become much more apparent to the child. They will better understand the experiences of the harmed individual and develop the necessary empathy.

Remind children that when they are online, they may sometimes easily forget that the person on the other side is a human being. According to the media equation theory (Reeves & Nass, 1996), our brains evolved before the existence of the internet, so our brain might make mistakes because it struggles to adapt to these new conditions. It is important to always remind children that the individuals they interact with, in the online space, are real people, not just usernames and bodyless profile pictures. While the internet has many advantages, it often leads to dehumanization, especially when we don't personally know the individual, causing us to forget that they are a human being with their own emotions and unique personality, and they may also be vulnerable.

Remind children that they should not disclose anything online that they wouldn't say face-to-face in the offline world. It's important to emphasize that online communications are always recordable and retrievable, and unethical behavior committed online may be used against them in the future. Although many unethical actions may not be illegal, there is no reason to disregard them simply because they are not against the law.

It is crucial that we uphold the same standards in the online world as we do in the offline world. Simply put, we must stand against hate speech, abuse of children, and plagiarism in the online environment, just as we do against unethical behaviors in the offline world. Values such as goodwill, kindness, openness, and respect for others should be promoted in online space. We need to remind children that theft, harm to individuals, and bullying, even if carried out online, are still equivalent to theft, and bullying in the real world. For instance, reading someone's emails without their permission is equivalent to opening and reading a letter that belongs to someone else in their mailbox.

Remind children don't make a permanent decision based on a temporary emotion. Encourage them to give themselves some time to calm down and try to have offline conversations with the individuals involved when they are calmer. If their friends have posted something or shared a photo that they didn't like on social media, avoid seeking revenge by sharing their private photos that were previously sent to them. Discourage them from speaking ill of others or retaliating and advise them not to encourage their friends to attack them.

The online environment is a space where differences between individuals are more pronounced compared to the offline world. In the offline world, we have friends who look like us. We live in a place where people are generally homogenous and share a common language with those around us. However, in the online world, due to the breaking down of barriers, we encounter a multitude of individuals and groups who are different from us. These individuals and groups may sometimes seem strange, ignorant, or even antagonistic to us. Open-mindedness and tolerance for diverse and opposing beliefs are essential traits in the online space. Lack of open-mindedness prevents us from engaging with different perspectives in the online sphere.

However, in the online space, despite the potential for engaging with groups with different perspectives, individuals tend to exhibit the same habits they have offline, gravitating toward people who are like themselves. They befriend those who resemble them, follow those who share similar beliefs, and engage in conversations with those who hold similar convictions. In this regard, there is a theory known as the "Echo Chamber" (Cinelli et al., 2021) which metaphorically represents a situation where only certain opinions and beliefs are reinforced.

It's as if we are in a room where we only hear our own voices. In other words, we selectively pursue sources that reinforce our own beliefs rather than challenging ones that may contradict or challenge our views. We interact with specific individuals who are similar to us and, in a way, find ourselves in a chamber that incessantly repeats information that aligns with our beliefs and convictions. Due to our inclination to listen to like-minded ideas and the reluctance to engage with opposing viewpoints in the online space, we create a loop of friends, media outlets, and pages that constantly reinforce our own beliefs. This hinders the opportunity to hear diverse opinions that could contribute to our intellectual and cognitive growth. Therefore, it is crucial to be open-minded and expose us to different and even conflicting perspectives in the online sphere.

When using technology and the virtual space at home, it is important to have specific ethical guidelines and adhere to them. Additionally, engage in discussions with children about morally controversial topics, such as incidents occurring at school or in the news. For example, disseminating private photos of an actor, a writer suing a director for copyright violation, inappropriate behavior of an influencer toward their followers, and so on.

During web browsing and the use of social media, children might encounter inappropriate content that contain insults toward ethnicities, races, religions, women, LGPTQs, etc. As responsible adults, it is important for us to express our disapproval of such content to them and teach them to respect differences. This way, they can act ethically and responsibly as digital citizens in the online space.

Teach children that they can report or flag inappropriate and offensive content in the online environment. When we come across offensive comments or inappropriate posts on social media, we can report them. Social networking platforms like Telegram, Facebook, Instagram, and others will block users or channels that have produced inappropriate content if the report is valid.

We should teach children that by creating content in the online space, they are actively participating in shaping the culture of society, and they should not underestimate their role in this regard. Therefore, they should consider the influence their generated content has on the audience and the societal culture.

Accept the mistakes of children. As the saying goes, "someone who makes no mistakes makes nothing at all," but we should always respond to unethical behavior.

Educate Children to Know Their Rights in Online Space

I have heard numerous stories about people who have been threatened with the disclosure of their chats or private information by someone. At least once, we might have witnessed online threats made by individuals. We have seen how people defame each other, whether with known identities or anonymously, without any fear of legal consequences or punishment, as they believe they are completely immune. In this situation the victims often feel helpless in dealing with such behavior.

Unfortunately, among the primary victims in this context can be adolescents and sometimes are unaware of their rights, making them susceptible to exploitation. Hence, it is imperative for individuals, especially parents, to have knowledge and awareness about the rights and responsibility of users in the online environment, so they can educate their children about these regulations.

We are not defenceless in the online realm, and in fact, there are laws that we need to be acquainted with to be able to defend ourselves in specific circumstances. These laws, pertaining to cybercrime, are part of media literacy knowledge. As active users of communication technologies, children should be aware of their rights. They should understand what actions in the online space, which is quite extensive, are considered criminal according to the law and what penalties are associated with them. This knowledge will prevent them from committing crimes and enable them to protect themselves and those around them by utilizing the assistance of the law in sensitive situations.

References

Bandura, A. (1989). Social cognitive theory. In R. Vasta (Ed.), *Annals of child development. Vol. 6. Six theories of child development* (pp. 1–60). Greenwich, CT: JAI Press.

Cinelli, M., De Francisci Morales, G., Galeazzi, A., Quattrociocchi, W., & Starnini, M. (2021). The echo chamber effect on social media. *Proceedings of the National Academy of Sciences*, 118(9), np. https://doi.org/10.1073/pnas.2023301118

Hinduja, S. (2021). *Cyberbullying atatistics 2021 | age, gender, sexual orientation, and race*. Cyberbullying Research Center. Retrieved May 2024, from https://rb.gy/lhqum0

Kohlberg, L. & Hersh, R. H. (1977). Moral development: A review of the theory. *Theory into Practice*, 16(2), 53–59.

Mediasmarts (n.d). *How kids cyberbully*. Mediasmarts; Canada's Centre for Digital Media Literacy. Retrieved February 2023 from https://mediasmarts.ca/digital-media-literacy/digital-issues/cyberbulling/how-kids-cyberbully

Olson, K. R., & Shaw, A. (2010). 'No fair, copycat!': What children's response to plagiarism tells us about their understanding of ideas. *Developmental Science*, 14(2), 431–439. https://doi.org/10.1111/j.1467-7687.2010.00993.x

Reeves, B., & Nass, C. (1996). *Media equation*. Retrieved June 2023, from http://www.uky.edu/~drlane/capstone/mass/equation.htm

Roth-Hanania, R. (2002). The role of self-concept development in the devel-opment of empathic concern during infancy. *ETD Collection for Fordham University*. Retrieved 2009, from http://fordham.bepress.com/dissertations/AAI3037228

Smith, P. K., Mahdavi, J., Carvalho, M., Fisher, S., Russell, S., & Tippett, N. (2008). Cyberbullying: Its nature and impact in secondary school pupils. *Journal of Child Psychology and Psychiatry*, 49(4), 376–385.

Tan, L., Volling, B. L., Gonzalez, R., LaBounty, J., & Rosenberg, L. (2021). Growth in emotion understanding across early childhood: A cohort-sequential model of firstborn children across the transition to siblinghood. *Child Development*, 93(3), e299–e314. https://doi.org/10.1111/cdev.13729. Epub 2021 Dec 31.

7 Improving Children's Advertisement Literacy

Inoculate Children against Advertisements

Advertisements are everywhere. They are on the streets, at home, on toys, on television—basically, everywhere. There is always a message somewhere urging us to engage in a particular action, thought, or feeling. When we lack sufficient advertisement literacy, we should question whether we truly have control over ourselves or not. This issue is even bigger when it comes to children. They have not yet gained enough experience to understand advertisements and the intentions behind them. Therefore, it is crucial to teach them to think critically about advertisements. Advertisements could have a significant influence on children's behavior as consumers. Consequently, one of the objectives of media literacy education is to transform children into discerning consumers.

A discerning consumer is someone who:

- Understands and expresses their preferences and desires.
- Explores various methods to fulfill those desires, including researching products and services.
- Selects and purchases a product based on informed decision-making.
- Evaluates the purchased product as well as alternative.
- Acquires knowledge, skills, and appropriate behavior to function as a discerning consumer.

When educating children about advertisements, it is important to remember that advertising has two dimensions: rhetoric and aesthetics. The rhetorical aspect pertains to the art of persuasion used to convince the audience. The aesthetic aspect encompasses all the audio, written, and visual techniques employed to enhance the attractiveness of advertisements. Advertisers often enlist the talents of artists and creative individuals to craft their advertising messages, showcasing their own artistry within the realm of advertising. Familiarity with the art used in advertising helps children develop an appreciation for beauty and nurtures their creativity. It is essential to reinforce a

DOI: 10.4324/9781003528685-8

child's aesthetic sensibility; advertisements provide a great opportunity for us to do so. Children need to understand that the beauty of an advertisement and its message delivery are separate from the quality of the product being advertised. To guide children in adopting a critical and aesthetic approach to advertisements, we must first understand their perception and comprehension of advertising.

Studies of children indicate that those below the ages of 4–5 years do not consistently distinguish program from commercial content, even when program/commercial separation devices are used. As children reach the age of 4–5 years, they typically perceive a categorical distinction between commercials and programming, but primarily on the basis of affective ("commercials are funnier") or perceptual ("commercials are shorter") cues only (Wilcox et al., 2004). However, children older than 5 perceive advertisements in the following manner:

- They are able to distinguish between advertisements and other programs but are unaware that the advertisement is attempting to sell a product.
- They find advertising programs appealing and entertaining, enjoying watching them.
- Generally, they do not have a discerning or critical perspective toward advertisements and advertisers.

Basic developmental research on egocentrism and perspective taking, along with a great deal of evidence specifically examining developmental differences in the comprehension of persuasive intent within advertisements, establishes clearly that most children younger than 78 years of age do not recognize the persuasive intent of commercial appeals (Wilcox et at., 2004). The comprehension of children aged 7–11 regarding advertisements can be summarized as follows:

- They can discern that advertisements are attempting to sell a product.
- They can remember advertising messages.
- They can recognize certain advertising techniques.
- They may not always have a critical perspective toward advertisements.
- They may not be able to distinguish whether the products are as good as portrayed in the advertisements.

Young children, up to the age of 3, often engage in the most intense conflicts with their parents over purchasing items they see in television advertisements or stores. They resort to shouting, crying, or even becoming aggressive, if necessary, in order to persuade their parents to buy what they want.

If parents give in to these tactics, children will not seek alternative approaches and will always attempt to fulfill their desires through shouting and demanding. However, if parents do not give in to their demands, children will try to find new ways to persuade their parents.

In essence, they sit at the negotiation table and try to convince you through bargaining. Surrendering to a child's screams deprives them of the opportunity to think of other creative ways to persuade you. At this stage, you can express the reasons for not making the purchase through conversation, listen to your child's reasons, and ultimately resolve the issue in a logical and peaceful manner.

It is important to consistently maintain this approach. Your child may not give up this behavior for a while, but do not lose hope. Eventually, the child will be influenced and accept your approach. This approach will help them become rational in adulthood and act logically and thoughtfully in response to their inner desires.

To foster critical thinking in children regarding advertisements, consider the following:

- First and foremost, it is important to help children distinguish advertisements from other programs.
- To do this, it is better to ask them about the differences between advertisements and other programs, engaging them in question-centered conversations to help them understand the distinction.
- Discuss different types of advertisements with your child. When you come across billboard or poster advertisements, ask their opinion on whether they find the advertisement appealing.
- While watching an advertisement, you can ask your child what they think the advertisement wants them to do, to think or feel about. Encourage them to express their thoughts and emotions.

You should help them to differentiate between commercial and non-commercial advertisements. Commercial advertisements aim to sell a product, while non-commercial advertisements serve purposes such as raising awareness about diseases, health, social relationships, religion, etc.

This differentiation should also be approached through examples and in the form of conversational and question-centered interactions. Try to lead the conversation in a way that encourages the child to think and try to discover the differences between these two types of advertisements.

Discuss with the child the impact of using music in advertisements on people's emotions and feelings. You can ask them to share their feelings when a musical advertisement is played. The goal of this conversation should be to raise their awareness of their emotions while watching the advertisement and to understand that people can be influenced by advertisements.

One of the stimuli that can motivate our minds is creative and innovative advertisements that break the structure, defamiliarize, and offer a different perspective on what we commonly see. Therefore, while we can critically analyze the message of these advertisements, the way they present the message can serve as a valuable stimulus for stimulating children's creativity.

Introduce various types of commercial and non-commercial advertisements to your child, such as written, visual, audio-visual, etc. After watching the advertisements together with your child, you can ask them the following questions:

- What is the objective of this advertisement? Who do you think are the creators of this advertisement?
- Who are the intended audience of this advertisement?
- How do they try to convince us to spend our money on purchases or, for example, pay attention to a UNICEF advertisement (an example of non-commercial advertisement) and change our behavior?
- Do you think they are able to change your mind?
- What assumptions exist in this advertisement, and are their assumptions true?
- What techniques have they used in these advertisements to persuade us?
- In their opinion, at what time of the day should these advertisements be broadcast in order to reach the largest audience?

Common Advertising Techniques

To educate your child about advertisements, it is important for you to be aware of advertising techniques so that you can help your child identify them. These techniques are numerous, and we encounter new variations of them every day, as creativity plays a significant role in this industry. That is why organizations and companies constantly create new ways to influence their audience. You can find reliable sources to learn about advertising techniques. However, below, I have provided examples of some of the most common techniques used in both commercial and non-commercial advertisements.

Relying on Emotions

This advertising technique is performed using two factors: the customer's needs and fears. People generally have common needs, such as the need for new experiences, the need for being accepted in groups, communities, and society, the need to be seen or recognized, or the need for security. However, fear is also an emotion in humans and can be used as another advertising tool. For example, fear of accidents, fear of death, fear of being overlooked, fear of illness, or fear of aging. Advertisers, knowing these needs and fears, present and introduce their products, services, or goods in a way that addresses one or more human needs or fears. They might promote themselves in a way that if customers use their products, they will, for example, appear youthful or will be immune to illness.

Promotional Advertisement

In this technique, advertising aims to capture the attention of its audience toward its products or services. For example, they offer items or services for free to individuals. These items or services are provided to potential customers on various occasions, such as festivals or holidays, at multiple locations, in order to attract the attention of different audiences.

Encourage to Conformity

In this type of technique, potential customers are encouraged to purchase the product and be part of the crowd like others; in fact, they leverage the human inclination to belong to a group and be part of a community. For example, they may state "two million people have trusted us. What about you"?

Presenting Numbers

In this technique, advertisers use numbers, symbols, and real-life examples to demonstrate the quality of their product. For instance, they may say that our products are recommended by 80% of doctors.

Affirmation

In this technique, famous or prominent individuals are used to advertise a product and they provide their endorsement, affirming that the product is the best. Experts may also be employed to validate the product. Occasionally, a person dressed as a dentist may be employed to promote a toothpaste, for example.

Customer Praise

In this approach, advertisers create the impression that because you deserve, you use our products. For example, they might say, "You drive a Toyota because you deserve the best."

Ideal Family

Advertisers employ this technique to convey that families and children who use their products are happy. The homes of these families, as depicted in advertisements, are always clean and organized, and their children are joyful and beautiful. By showcasing this family, it is implicitly suggested that if you use our product, you will become an ideal family.

Exaggeration

Exaggeration is heavily used in advertising because it is both captivating and more likely to be remembered by the audience. Advertisers often employ special effects to exaggerate certain features of a product, such as appearance, size, beauty, scent, or functionality. For example, claiming that the scent of an air freshener can reach another country or that the speed of a car exceeds the speed of sound.

Repetition

In this technique, a sentence or phrase is repeated extensively, often accompanied by music or catchy jingles, to make it memorable and have an impact on the audience.

As I mentioned, advertising techniques are countless, and their number continues to grow every day. It's important for you to be able to recognize these techniques and discuss them with children as well.

Improving Children's Critical Thinking toward Political Advertising

It is not the case that political advertising solely targets adults; depending on the circumstances and subject matter, political advertising can also target children. On the other side, the target audience of the advertising campaign may be adults, but children can still be influenced by exposure to these advertisements. Therefore, it is necessary to raise children's awareness not only about commercial and non-commercial advertising but also about political advertising.

In the current era that controlling the flood of information toward children is challenging, it is necessary to familiarize them with political advertising and educate children on how to protect themselves. As parents, it is important for you to assist your child in not only reading the lines but also understanding between the lines and becoming aware of how advertising can impact their judgments.

The most crucial clue to identifying the instrumental use of children in advertising is their involvement in advertisements unrelated to the child and their issues. For example:

- When participating in a campaign supporting a candidate and encouraging your child to carry a symbol of support for that candidate or attaching it to them.

- Posting an image of your child or any other child with a specific sign in your online social media profile or page to advertise a candidate or any other political figure.
- The child wearing a headband with a political slogan or statement unrelated to children, and so on.
- Employing children to advocate for political causes that they may not fully understand or have a personal connection to.
- In all these situations, you are exploiting the child. If such uses of children's images occur in media advertising, it is referred to as the objectification or exploitation of children in advertising.

What to Do?

To raise awareness of your child about political advertising, engage them in discussions about the messages conveyed in political advertisements. Explain to your child how a candidate's message may be completely contradictory to their actual actions. Additionally, talk to your child about the power of charisma. Help them understand that a candidate having a pleasant smile, or an attractive face does not necessarily make them a good person or a suitable candidate.

It is important to protect children from political advertising; however, involving children over the age of 12 in political activities to familiarize them with the realm they will encounter in the future is good. Here, we need to distinguish between the concepts of "targeting children" and "raising children's awareness." The aim is to prevent them from becoming targets of political advertising; and doing activities that make them aware of political advertising techniques. Here are some tips:

- Talk to your child about the impact of using music in advertisements on people's emotions and feelings. You can ask them to discuss their emotions when watching a commercial with a jingle. The purpose of this conversation should be making your child aware of their emotions while watching a commercial and help them understand that they may be influenced by the music or other elements of the commercial.
- Discuss filming techniques with your child; how camera angles can make someone appear big and powerful, or conversely, how choosing a certain camera angle can ignore and not show significant aspects of reality.
- Engage in a discussion about advertising messages, focusing on how one can determine whether they will adhere to their promises or not. Furthermore, explore whether these advertising promises are relevant to their work or not.
- If you hold a dissenting view or consider a candidate's advertising approach to be negative, talk to your child about the reasons for your disagreement and inquire about their opinion on the matter.

- The charisma of an individual has the potential to influence us all. Discuss with your child the concept of charisma and provide practical examples of how a person's voice or appearance can affect our emotions, leading us to make irrational and emotion-driven decisions.

Engage in a discussion about your concerns within the relevant domain and ask your child to talk about their concerns, focusing on whether the preferred candidate addresses those concerns or not. For example, guide your child's attention toward whether a candidate talks about environmental protection, gender equality, etc., discuss the significance of the slogans they put forth and how they may reflect the candidate's genuine concerns and approach.

It is crucial to differentiate between these two scenarios: whether children's participation in political advertisements is aimed at involving them in activities relevant to their interests (such as a candidate discussing children's concerns and desires) or if they are merely being exploited for advertising purposes. Have a conversation with your child about these two situations. When they understand the distinction between these two situations, they will likely never allow others to exploit them for advertising purposes.

The purpose of these conversations, in addition to raising awareness about advertising, is to make them interested in social engagement. Also, the aim is not to involve them heavily in politics, but rather to familiarize their minds with relevant issues and concepts in this domain. The most important point to consider in these conversations is to avoid assuming that the child is a passive individual. Instead, these discussions should ideally be participatory and structured in a "dialogue" format.

Reference

Wilcox, B. L., Kunkel, D., Cantor, J., Dowrick, P., Linn, S., & Palmer, E. (2004). *Report of the APA task force on advertising and children*. American Psychological Association. Retrieved June 2023, from https://shorturl.at/iqIK2

8 Media and Child Sexual Education

Sex Education by Media

Research indicates that children sometimes use the internet to search for information related to sexual matters (Buhi et al., 2009). The issue is that what children typically find on the internet in this regard is an unhealthy response to their healthy curiosity.

The best approach in dealing with children regarding this subject is to acknowledge that their curiosity about sexual matters is normal and natural. Therefore, it is important to gain their trust and enhance their critical thinking skills. These skills will help them make appropriate decisions in the online environment and engage in healthy behavior.

One of the primary sources children primarily turn to in order to satisfy their sexual curiosity is the internet. Based on my experience of talking to parents, after the age of 7, children may search for keywords related to sexual anatomy on the internet, and as they grow older, these searches become more specialized and can potentially lead them to pornographic content.

Media can significantly influence children's sexual development and shape their understanding of gender. They can convey messages about how girls and boys should generally behave or teach them about sexual behavior through pornography and represent them as normal behavior.

According to sexual script theory (Gagnon & Simon, 1973) which was initially developed to explain the impact of sexual content in traditional media,

> its tenets can also be adopted to explore the implications of sexual messages in the digital environment. Within the context of digital media uses, sexual script theory argues that online sexual content is stored in users' memories and operates as a script to guide their future sexual behaviour. For example, when digital media users observe how other couples behave on social media (e.g., expressing their love for each other), they can store this information and use it to guide their (online) behaviours within a romantic relationship.
>
> (Maes et al., 2022)

DOI: 10.4324/9781003528685-9

If parents and teachers are absent in discussing sexual matters and providing meaningful guidance in this area for children, the impact of media on children's sexual development is inevitable and it will be the media that play an important intermediary role in providing meaning and understanding of these subjects.

Stating that a 7-year-old child should be knowledgeable about healthy sexual behavior, healthy sexual relationships, sexually transmitted diseases, pregnancy prevention methods, and so on does not imply that we are giving them permission to engage in sexual behavior. Rather, the point here is that we must make every effort to become the primary source for shaping a child's attitudes and beliefs about sexual matters, ensuring that their initial understanding is formed through us before potentially unhealthy intermediaries such as media or peers convey them unhealthy perspectives.

The reason for this concern is that a child's initial perceptions and attitudes about healthy sexual behavior are formed during the ages of 7–9. That is the reason why we must take seriously the first curiosity of children about sexual relationships. It's crucial for children to understand what makes a healthy sexual relationship and how to approach it, as it affects their current and future well-being, shaping their attitudes and behaviors positively. Therefore, during this sensitive period, we must utilize various opportunities to engage in conversations with children about sexual matters and explain sexual relationships as act based on love, commitment, and responsibility.

Your child may come across pornography videos at school or through their friends' mobile devices, which can completely confuse or frighten them. We need to empower children to handle such situations. Research indicates that one in ten children have watched pornography by the time they are 9 years old (Taylor, 2023) and in the absence of healthy sources, these explicit materials shape their perception of sexual behavior. Therefore, it is crucial to engage in open discussions with them about these topics.

Media can be terrifying or bewildering for children and may encourage them to engage in sexual activities before they are ready. While it is essential to ensure that children are not exposed to pornographic content, there is no guarantee that we can completely protect them from accessing such material. Therefore, the best approach is to provide them with sufficient knowledge in this area.

Children above the ages of 11 or 12, who have developed their capacity for ethical reasoning, possess the ability to engage with sexual or violent content in a thoughtful manner. This is why critical discussions and genuine participation in such issues help them become sensitive to these matters and develop a contextual understanding.

Media's Influence on Relationship and Sexual Behaviors

Media, through its sexual content, can influence children's attitudes toward relationships and sexual behaviors, shaping potentially destructive and unrealistic perspectives. For example, when they see a woman being forced into a sexual encounter and seemingly enjoying it in a film, they may perceive such behavior as acceptable for women. Risky and unsafe sexual relationships are often portrayed in an attractive manner in the media, leading children and adolescents to believe that such behaviors are normal and have no negative consequences.

Research indicates that continuous exposure to pornography can lead to decreased empathy (Kor et al., 2022) toward women and encourage the viewer see them as mere objects. Similarly, women may also start seeing themselves as objects.

Films and online images often objectify women, exaggerate sexual encounters, lack emotional depth in their portrayals, and present sexual relationships solely for pleasure, while depicting men with six-pack abs and women as idealized models. These influences have a significantly negative impact on children, to the extent that they may become dissatisfied with their own bodies.

Pornography is an overly simplified, exaggerated, and glamorized form of fantasy entertainment. Porn stars can appear flawless and perfect. Pornography tends to be male-centric, produced by men, and often lacks acknowledgment of women's sexual desires and respect for their autonomy. This type of sexual relationship can serve as a model in the minds of girls, defining success in sexual encounters based on this distorted representation, allowing objectification, and enabling exploitation by men.

To promote critical thinking in children regarding sexual content in media you can consider following tips:

- Engage in open and honest conversations with your child, based on reality and without embarrassment.
- Help your child understand the harmful effects of images that objectify or degrade women, as well as images that pressure boys to conform to a hypersexualized and masculine ideal of attractiveness and power. Use examples from movies or media to illustrate these concepts. Children gradually learn to think critically about any image portrayed in the media.
- Discuss healthy and normal expressions of sexuality, as well as the destructive ones that exist online.
- If children consistently hear from their caregivers that sexual desires are closely connected to love, respect, and affectionate relationships, they will recognize the unrealistic nature of pornography.

If you notice that your child has been searching for pornographic content online, do not panic. While they should not be exposed to pornographic films, their curiosity is natural and similar to young children's interest in watching scary movies that frighten them, but they repeatedly watch. Many children watch those horrifying scenes multiple times because they are emotionally and psychologically affected by the content. Therefore, they attempt to understand and gain control over those feelings by repeatedly watching horrifying scenes.

Explain to them that just like their favorite movies, pornography is a film that exaggerates and portrays sexual relationships as completely superficial. Tell them that what they have seen are scripted stories, and the actors in those films are paid for their performances and actions. Have a discussion with them about the signs of healthy sexual behavior, such as intimacy, commitment, consent, and responsibility in sexual relationships. These concepts are rarely depicted in the media, but they are incredibly important in real life.

All in all, if you discover that your child has searched for sexual content, follow these steps:

- Don't make your child feel guilty about their feelings and sexual inclinations. Be more of a trusted source for them rather than a moral authority.
- Avoid punishing them. Punishment won't stop them from seeking sexual information; instead, it will likely push them to engage in such activities covertly. Have a conversation with them and respond to any questions they have through an inquiry-based discussion.
- Be aware that your child is curious. When faced with such a situation, don't immediately jump to the worst-case scenario. It's better to understand that your child has taken a step into a new territory or is experimenting with something unfamiliar, so they're trying to figure it out.
- Have an honest conversation with your child. Show them that you are neither embarrassed nor judgmental about their curiosity. Avoid portraying their actions as naughty or bad, as it can harm them. Let them know that they can always come to you and ask their questions. We should raise them in a way that enables them to protect themselves from engaging in harmful behaviors.

Keep in mind that early sexual behaviors in children are not sufficient or accurate indicators of their future sexual experiences. Parents should not view children's sexual behaviors through the lens of an adult.

References

Buhi, E. R., et al. (2009). An observational study of how young people search for online sexual health information. *Journal of American College Health*, 58, 101–111.

Gagnon, J. H., & Simon, W. (1973). *Sexual conduet: The social sources of human sexuality*. Chicago, IL: Aldine.

Kor, A., Djalovski, A., Potenza, M. N., Zagoory-Sharon, O., & Feldman, R. (2022). Alterations in oxytocin and vasopressin in men with problematic pornography use: The role of empathy. *Journal of Behavioral Addictions*, 11(1), 116–127. https://doi.org/10.1556/2006.2021.00089

Maes, C., van Oosten, J. M. F., & Vandenbosch, L. (2022). Adolescents' digital media interactions within the context of sexuality development. In J. Nesi, E. H. Telzer, & M. J. Prinstein (Eds.), *Handbook of adolescent digital media use and mental health* (pp. 135–161). Cambridge University Press. Cambridge, UK.

Taylor, L. (2023). One in 10 children 'have watched pornography by time they are nine'. *The Guardian*. Retrieved from https://www.theguardian.com/society/2023/jan/31/one-in-10-children-have-watched-pornography-by-time-they-are-nine

9 Teenagers and Online Space

Teenagers Access to Online Space

If your 12-year-old child is using the internet for chat with stranger, there's no need to worry. Your child is entering the stage of adolescence, and establishing connections at this phase is a crucial part of their personal development and social life. They are preparing for independence and gradually distancing from you. Chatting aligns with their need to understand society and engage with it. If they navigate toward this capability on the internet, they are progressing through their developmental stages normally.

Assist them in utilizing this capability for their growth without harm, following these tips:

- Educate them about online risks. Let them know that similar to the offline world, there are individuals who can steal personal information or photos and use them to blackmail or exploit others. They may even publish personal photos of you on the internet for their own pleasure.
- Advise them not to share personal information on any website or click on any suspicious or untrustworthy link, as it can lead to data theft or expose them to malware.
- Encourage them to be cautious in trusting those they chat with online. They should refrain from sending personal photos or any information that could cause trouble for their future if it were to be circulated on the internet.
- Advise them not to send photos or information to classmates or friends that could have serious consequences if shared online. Warn them that their friends may not be responsible or trustworthy enough in safeguarding those photos or information.
- Remind them that the information they post on the internet remains there indefinitely. They should be cautious about sharing information that could create a negative image of them if, for example, they apply for a job ten years later and their potential employer comes across that content.

DOI: 10.4324/9781003528685-10

- Get to know your child's interests. Let them know that they can connect with like-minded individuals on the internet and learn from them in their areas of interest.
- Introduce them to social media pages and communities that align with their interests.
- Make them aware of the negative effects of prolonged use of communication technologies on their well-being. They should learn to manage their media consumption time themselves.

Your child may be inclined to engage in chats about content that you may not approve of. You are understandably concerned about potential harm they may encounter, so have an open conversation with them about those risks. Enable them to protect themselves against those risks and help them utilize the internet consciously, not merely driven by their impulses.

Parents Have a Louder Voice

Parents need to be aware that in today's era, photoshopped celebrities and famous influencers can set beauty standards for children before they realize they are not real. Children do not refrain from watching movies or using social media platforms. That's why parents should help children decode films and advertisements, critically look at social media and question the conveyed messages.

Parents should educate their children about the concept of representation, allowing them to enjoy watching movies while being aware of misleading representations. Although teenagers may claim to be aware of such misrepresentations, it cannot be assumed that they are immune to their influence solely based on awareness.

It can be argued that adolescents are more vulnerable compared to other age groups because they are in the process of developing a solid understanding of their identity and may lack stability in their sense of self. Therefore, if they resemble beautiful actors in movies, they feel valued, whereas otherwise, they may feel worthless.

There are numerous obstacles in helping adolescents avoid comparing themselves to celebrities and actors because these values have infiltrated societies with the help of art. We are all aware that the images portrayed in the media are representations of reality, not reality itself. However, the standards of beauty we hold in our minds largely correspond with what is portrayed in the media. These standards are reproduced in society, and adolescents are also influenced by them.

Nevertheless, it is still the parents who can assist adolescents in perceiving their self-worth independent of the influence of media representations. Parental guidance is a process that begins from early childhood, encompassing the behaviors they exhibit toward their child and, most importantly, the behaviors they exhibit toward themselves. For instance, when a parent express dissatisfaction with their bodies and constantly worry about weight gain or skin aging, they unintentionally instil in their children the notion that physical appearance is crucial for happiness. Building upon this foundation, the media can influence adolescents, capitalizing on the prerequisites of happiness that become intertwined with physical appearance, thereby reinforcing the narrative of the beauty and fashion industry.

The most important aspect for parents to consider is not just looking outward and worrying about the messages their child receives, but also paying attention to themselves and the messages they convey to their child. The schemas are created in a child's mind under the influence of interactions with others, particularly parents, that shape the trajectory of the child's life in the future.

Reducing the Pressure of Social Media on Adolescents

From the age of 11 or 12, children, due to their age and developmental stage, become interested in social media. They gradually distance themselves from their parents and seek to engage and interact with society. Becoming interested in social media aligns with this development.

Despite the positive aspects that social media networks can offer to children, such as enhancing their social skills, exposure to others' thoughts and beliefs, increasing tolerance for different viewpoints, finding shared concepts and meanings with other individuals in the community, they can also impose significant pressure on adolescents. They can diminish their self-confidence and evoke negative emotions arising from comparing themselves to others.

Encountering exaggerated images of happiness and beauty on social media platforms instils a sense of falling behind in children, adolescents, and adults. It also triggers negative emotions and diminishes their self-confidence. This impact can be more detrimental to adolescents as they have less experience and, consequently, possess fewer conceptual tools to resist these negative emotions.

However, how can we assist adolescents in avoiding the negative influence of social media? There are some tips as follows:

- Encourage them to think critically about posts they see on social media platforms, and when discussing social media with them, encourage them to have a critical perspective. For example, ask them to consider what might have been cropped or edited in the images they see on social media, and why. This question can lead to larger inquiries such as whether they believe the individuals represented online are the same in the offline world, including themselves. What is the purpose of sharing a photo? Do Likes give them a sense of validation? Does reading posts on social media affect their mood?

- Model appropriate reactions to failure for them. On social media, failures are not often showcased, leading us to witness others' successes without seeing their struggles. Children should understand that experiencing failure is not inherently negative. If parents do not talk to their children about their own failures and share their experiences, children will only expect successes in their life, not failures. Show your children that failures teach us how to succeed and that we should not be ashamed of them.

Take social media seriously. Adolescents who are just stepping into social media have not experienced life without them, and comments, likes, images, etc., are completely real to them. Therefore, take the time to engage in conversations with them about online space.

Keep in mind that stopping teenagers' internet use does not protect them from the drawbacks of social media. Research indicates that stopping teenagers' internet usage not only fails to safeguard them from the negative effects of social media but may also hinder their digital skill development and prevent them from building sufficient emotional resilience. In fact, restricting children and adolescents from internet access deprives them of the opportunity to become familiar with online challenges and learn strategies to cope with them.

Social media platforms provide us with the opportunity to showcase our lives in an edited manner. This means that others only see the parts we choose to present. Based on this, occasionally explore popular profiles on platforms like Instagram or Facebook with your teenage child and critically examine their pages. This approach helps your child develop a critical perspective toward the representation of popular individuals on social media. Critical questions that can be the subject of discussion in this regard include:

- Are the photos posted by this individual authentic?
- How different can the real life of this person be from what we see?
- What kind of impact does this person have on their followers? Do you assess this impact as positive or negative?
- To what extent can social networks shape our perception of other peoples' lives, and how close can this perception be to reality?

It should be noted that the managed and purposeful use of the internet and social networks does not happen overnight. We need to be patient and think more about how we can use these technologies to improve our own skills and that of our children.

Index

Note: *Italic* page numbers refer to figures.

For Product Safety Concerns and Information please contact our EU representative GPSR@taylorandfrancis.com
Taylor & Francis Verlag GmbH, Kaufingerstraße 24, 80331 München, Germany

www.ingramcontent.com/pod-product-compliance
Lightning Source LLC
LaVergne TN
LVHW010936110826
845149LV00013B/2630

* 9 7 8 1 0 3 2 8 6 6 8 4 0 *